Pumping Nylon

In TAB

The Classical Guitarist's Technique Handbook

SCOTT TENNANT

Edited by Nathaniel Gunod

Alfred, the leader in educational publishing, and the
National Guitar Workshop, one of America's finest guitar schools,
have joined forces to bring you the best, most progressive
educational tools possible. We hope you will enjoy this book and
encourage you to look for other fine products from
Alfred and the National Guitar Workshop.

> ### for Joe Fava
> 1911–1994
> teacher and friend
>
> *"Composer, sculptor, painter, poet, prophet, sage,*
> *these are the makers of the after-world, the architects of heaven.*
> *The world is beautiful because they have lived;*
> *without them, laboring humanity would perish."*
> —James Allen
> from *As a Man Thinketh*

Acquisition, editorial, music typesetting and interior design: Nathaniel Gunod, Workshop Arts
Illustrations: Barbara Smolover, Workshop Arts
Cover photography: © Howard Sokol/Tony Stone Images • Guitar on cover by Richard Bruné

Table of Contents

Author's Preface

Welcome! This is my little book about guitar technique. I want to make it clear from the start that the material in this book is meant to reflect my own way of doing things on the instrument. The exercises are those that have helped me, some of which I still practice every day.

The goal of *Pumping Nylon* is to offer ideas that will help solve various technical problems. The idea was to steer clear of assembling anything that resembled a method book. Rather, my intent was to focus only on specific technical issues which I felt had not been clearly explained elsewhere. Generally, the issues dealt with in this book are those that have been brought up time and time again by students in master classes and lessons over the past ten years or so.

The exercises and musical examples have been chosen because of their unique technical challenges. For instance, the Bach *Double* was taken from a solo guitar arrangement, stripped of all its bass notes and more comfortable fingerings, and transformed into a very effective string-crossing and scale study.

I don't pretend to have addressed every issue. (There are too many out there for one book!) The reader, however, is strongly encouraged to invent his/her own exercises whenever necessary, since all of our technical needs are so very different.

I hope you find a few answers to some of your questions. Go get 'em!

I would like to thank ...

Nat Gunod, for coaching me through this process for the last two years; Brian Head and Andy York for composing their wonderful "made-to-order" etudes; Billy Arcila for posing for the photos that were used to create the illustrations; Durmel DeLeon for the photography; John Dearman and Matt Greif for their technical assistance; an endless list of friends for their constant encouragement; and the students at the National Guitar Summer Workshop, San Francisco Conservatory and the University of Southern California for being (not always voluntary) "guinea pigs" for much of the material contained herein.
And special thanks to Ron Krown at Alfred Publishing for encouraging us to do this new edition.

Glossary of Signs

This list will help you to interpret the various markings in the music.

1, 2, 3, 4	Left hand fingers, numbered from index (1) to pinky (4).
p, i, m, a,	Right hand fingers: *p* = thumb, *i* = index, *m* = middle, *a* = ring finger.
①②③④⑤⑥	The six strings of the guitar, numbered from low E ⑥ to high E ①.
IV, V, VII etc.	Roman numerals. Here is a quick review of these symbols: I=1, II=2, III=3, IV=4, V=5, VI=6, VII=7, VIII=8, IX=9, X=10, XI=11 and XII=12.
BII₄	The B indicates a barre. The Roman numeral indicates the fret to be barred, and the small subscript arabic numeral indicates the number of strings to be barred. So, this symbol would indicate to barre four strings at the second fret.
-1, -2, -3, -4	A dash in front of a fingering indicates a *guide finger shift*. A *shift* is a movement from one position to another. A *guide finger* is a finger that can be used just before and just after a shift. For instance, if the 4th finger has been used to play G on the 1st string, 3rd fret, and then moves to play A on the 1st string, 5th fret, it will be marked -4.

Editor's Preface

I hope you will enjoy this new edition of Scott's gratifyingly popular book. As a response to public demand, we are happy to provide a version of the book that includes tablature. Hopefully, this will make the book useful to more guitarists. After all, everyone who plays the guitar has something to gain from learning some classical guitar technique, and something to learn from a great teacher.

This book evolved from a warm-up routine and technical regimen that Scott Tennant began teaching and writing about several years ago. It is this daily warm-up that has inspired the whimsical title, *Pumping Nylon*. But in the following pages Scott has done far more than merely map out an exercise routine.

He has provided a wealth of technical information not readily available elsewhere. He has also compiled a variety of both well- and lesser-known technical exercises such as the *120 Right-Hand Studies* of Mauro Giuliani and some arpeggio studies by Francesco Tarrega, and has offered some exercises of his own as well. It is also through Scott Tennant that four great new studies, two by Brian Head and two by Andrew York, have been written and published.

But I think he has done a lot more than even those things.

What students and teachers alike will find in *Pumping Nylon* is a joyful attitude toward problem-solving on the classical guitar. There is an underlying message that says if you are willing and able to look at an issue from a different perspective, and if you can bring the same creative powers that you bring to your music-making to your technical work, you can overcome obstacles. Furthermore, there's no law that says it can't be fun.

Anyone who has studied classical guitar is going to find *something* in this book that directly contradicts what you have been taught—or what you teach—about *something*. This is inevitable. But if you dismiss this work for that reason, you will be missing much. I encourage you to read on. Take a look at all the ideas presented here by this great player and teacher. You will come away better for it.

I expect that for years to come it will be commonplace to find well-worn copies of this book in students' hands. I am sure that for Scott Tennant, as for myself, that will be the biggest reward for this effort.

Many thanks to the wonderful people at Alfred Publishing—especially the M.I. team—for helping to make this and many other National Guitar Workshop books a reality.

Nathaniel Gunod
Litchfield, Connecticut
July, 1997

Nathaniel Gunod has edited many guitar books including Benjamin Verdery's *Some Towns and Cities: The Solos*, *Renaissance Masters in TAB* by Howard Wallach, *Progressive Classical Solos* and *Play Along Library: Renaissance Duets*. He also co-authored Benjamin Verdery's instructional video, *The Essentials of Classical Guitar* and directed the video, *Pumping Nylon with Scott Tennant*. He is the author of *Classical Guitar for Beginners*. A recitalist on Baroque, Classical period and modern classical guitars, he has taught students from all over the world at the Peabody Conservatory of Music and the National Guitar Workshop, where he is Associate Director. He is the founder of the NGSW Classical Guitar Seminar and the D'Addario Guitar Concerto Competition.

How to Read Tablature

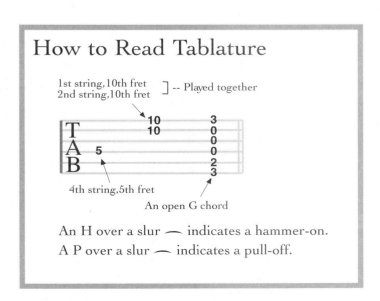

1st string, 10th fret
2nd string, 10th fret] -- Played together

4th string, 5th fret

An open G chord

An H over a slur ⌣ indicates a hammer-on.

A P over a slur ⌣ indicates a pull-off.

Some Do's and Don'ts

About the Hands

Before we immerse ourselves in the technical exercises in this book, let's cover some basics. There are numerous guitarists who, despite the seemingly awkward appearance of their hands, posture, and technique, produce amazing results. Generally, the philosophy is to leave well-enough alone (or, "if it ain't broke, don't fix it"). My original intention for this book was to avoid telling people exactly how to hold their hands, how to sit, etc. But there are some physical problems which one should avoid, and some basic truths that need to be addressed.

The hands should be in a constant state of *dynamic relaxation*. This means they should always be free of excess tension. At the same time, they should always be on stand-by; ready to play in an instant. Then they should empty, or relax, just as quickly. In order for all of this to happen, the hands need to be positioned as naturally as is possible while maintaining an advantageous angle to the strings.

For maximum results, the wrists of both the hands should be naturally straight (in relation to the arm), not forced into being straight. The diagrams below illustrate this point.

See here how the wrist is straight on the top-side of the hand, and not on the bottom-side.

Here the wrist is bent too much, and thus not allowing the tendons to work easily.

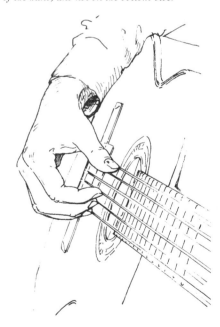
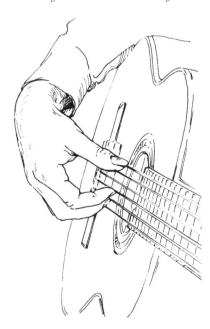

Try this experiment: keeping your wrist bent, make a fist. Not very comfortable, is it? In order for the fingers to work correctly, comfortably, and for extended periods of time, the tendons must be as free as possible to move around (like the cables that they are) inside the carpal tunnel. The carpal tunnel is the boney passage in your wrist. Bending the wrist too far aggravates the tendons, and could eventually cause irreparable damage.

In the two diagrams that follow, notice how the same principle applies to the left hand.

The straighter the wrist, the more dexterity your fingers will have.

Bending your wrist too much makes it a struggle to play

As for your left-hand thumb, it's generally wise to keep it positioned just under your second (middle) finger. This creates somewhat of a vise, and allows for an even distribution of pressure throughout the hand.

About the Body

The body should also be in a relaxed state. While seated, try stretching your neck and spine upwards towards the ceiling, pulling your shoulders back slightly (just enough to keep them from drooping forward). Now, relax your muscles so that your body sort of freezes itself in that position. This is a good state for the body to settle into. Your shoulders should not crunch upward into your neck. Take a look at the illustrations in the following section about holding the guitar.

About Holding the Guitar
—The Triangle

The guitar touches the body at three points to create a triangle:
1. At the lower part of the chest (near the sternum).
2. At the top of the left thigh.
3. At the inner part of the right thigh.

Of course, the reverse applies if you play left-handed! This triangle is held into place when the right forearm is rested on the instrument.

It's basic, yes, but this position provides the best angle for the guitar. For good tone production, especially in a concert situation, it is essential that the vibration of the back of the guitar is not compromised by placing it flat against your stomach. Since the guitar is such a directional instrument (it sounds best wherever you aim the soundhole), this angle also allows for the sound to travel a greater distance, because it keeps us from pointing the instrument at the floor.

"Failure to prepare is preparing to fail."

• John Wooden, former UCLA basketball coach •

The Left Hand

Finger Placement and Accuracy

It is vital to adopt a strong left-hand "stance" and place the fingers in a position which allows for maximum reach and flexibility.

As you can see from the illustration below, the fingers of the left hand are not all placed on the center of the fingertips. Rather, an advantageous position for the left hand is as follows:

1. The first finger (1) plays on the left side of its tip.
2. The second finger (2) plays just to the left of its tip.
3. The third finger (3) plays just to the right of its tip.
4. The fourth finger (4) makes contact on the right side of its tip.

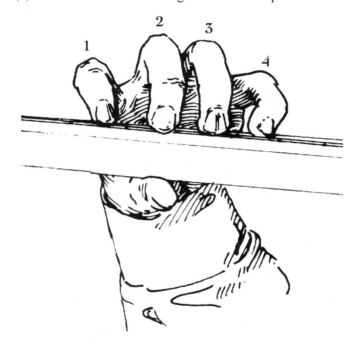

This position brings the larger muscles on either side of the hand into play, not necessarily to support fingers 1 and 4 (although this is a benefit), but to balance the whole hand and give it a stronger, more secure stance. It also allows for greater finger dexterity.

Notice the space between the middle joints of each finger. They're not touching! Not only are they not touching, but there is an intentional amount of extra space. This allows the fingers to spread apart and reach with greater speed when necessary. Never allow these joints to touch. This actually takes more muscular effort than keeping them apart, and the buzzword of this book is "economy": *economy of effort, economy of energy, economy of motion*.

As for the thumb, keep it just under the second finger. This helps to distribute the pressure evenly between the fingers and thumb, creating a sort of vise.

Pressure and Release

To familiarize yourself with this left-hand position, especially if it's new for you, practice the following.

Pressure/Release Exercise

Place your left hand in the correct position as shown on page 9. (Don't neglect your thumb, either.) Place fingers 1, 2, 3, and 4 on frets I, II, III, and IV respectively on any string (although I suggest you start with the third string ③). Press them down on the string and then *empty* them (release the pressure), keeping your fingers on the string. From this "relaxed-on-the-string" position, proceed to press the four fingers down, then empty them. Press, then empty. Press, then empty, and so on. Do this a number of times while keeping your fingers on the string. The point of this exercise is to feel the immediacy with which your fingers press (apply pressure), and then empty (totally release pressure) with the same immediacy. All four fingers should press and release simultaneously. Feel the vise grip we spoke of earlier. Feel the pressure distribute evenly throughout all four fingers and thumb.

After you have repeated this many times and gotten the hang of it, try it pressing the fingers down one at a time. Start from the same position as before: with all four fingers touching the string but not pressing.

Finger Exchange

As elementary as it may seem, we have just touched upon the most important issue concerning a good left hand: controlling the pressure and relaxation in the fingers. Now let's move on and approach exchanging fingers in the same manner.

The issue with exchanging fingers is maintaining the proper distance from the string. Notice in the illustration on the right that the fingers are all roughly the same distance to the string.

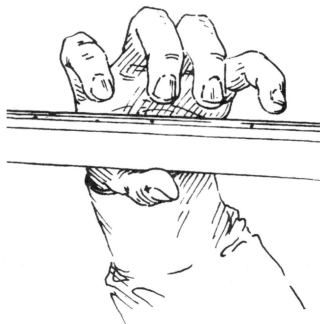

Ideally, the fingers should be about half an inch above the string, but definitely no more than one inch. Moving the fingers any farther than one inch above the string defeats our goal of economy of movement.

From this position, we will practice the following chromatic scale. With the same immediacy as in the previous drill, press the fingers down and empty them, one at a time, in order. This time, however, do not keep your fingers touching the string when not playing. When you empty a finger that has finished playing, spring it back into its place; about half an inch above the string. Since we will be dealing with the right hand in a later section, don't worry about which right-hand fingering to use for now. A simple *i, m* alternation will do. Use rest stroke or free stroke—it doesn't matter. Just focus on your left hand.

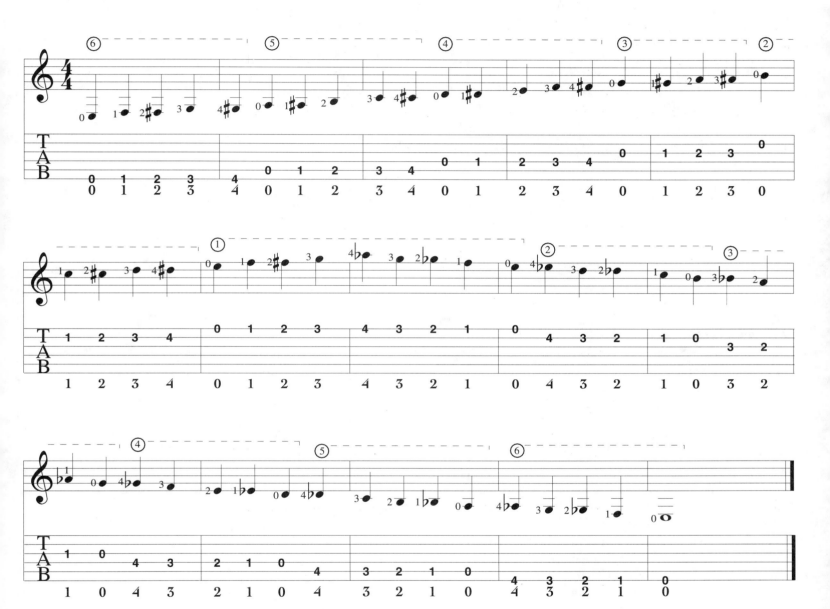

As one finger empties, make sure that the next *fills up* with exactly the same amount of pressure. I like to imagine this exchange as a shifting of weight from finger to finger. As you feel the weight shift, don't feel it only in the fingers, but throughout the whole hand. This will give you a heightened awareness of the balance in the hand.

Ascending Slurs (Hammer-ons)

A good, solid ascending slur (or, as it would lazily roll off our tongues in simpler times, "hammer-on") is nothing more than a slightly more energetic approach to the pressure/release applications.

From the half an inch hovering position pictured in the diagram on page 10, simply snap the desired finger onto the string. If you have diligently practiced the pressure/release exercises up until now, the feeling during execution of the slur is the same. The pressure is quick and accurate. In the case of the slur, the finger must be snapped down onto the string with slightly greater speed. This is what produces the sound and creates our tone during a slur. Don't think of bringing the finger up any further above the string than half an inch to an inch, or pressing down on the string any harder. The speed is what counts. I like to use the word "snap" when referring to a slur, because, for me, that's what it feels and sounds like.

In the following simple exercise, take your time and do several repetitions of each slur.

DO: snap the finger quickly and cleanly onto the string.
DON'T: continue to apply extra pressure once you're on the string.

If your slur is quick enough, the force with which you come down onto the string will be enough to keep the note sounding clearly.

Repeat each example at least 4x.

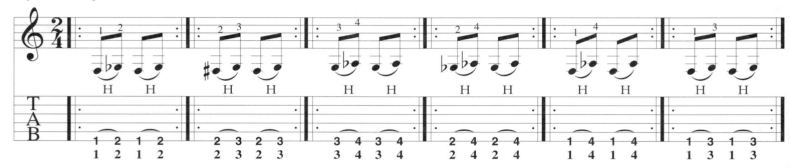

As in the pressure/release exercises, the shifting of weight from finger to finger is a must. Just before a finger executes its slur, it is empty. As it executes the slur, it fills up (with energy), and with a combination of muscle and weight (momentum), snaps onto the string; all in the blink of an eye.

Have faith! Work speed, not force and tension, into your slurs. And before you start complaining that half an inch is just not enough space, consider Bruce Lee's famous "One Inch Punch." With his fist only one inch away from his unfortunate volunteer's chest, he would punch, seeming only to tap the opposite fellow, and send him flying backwards for several yards! So, I think you can produce strong, clean-sounding slurs with a little less wind-up, don't you?

H = Hammer-on (ascending slur)
P = Pull-off (descending slur)

Descending Slurs (Pull-offs)

A descending slur, or pull-off, has the same sort of a "snap" to it, with only a few extra components.

In the two following illustrations, you can see what a secure pull-off looks like, and what an all too common but insecure pull-off looks like.

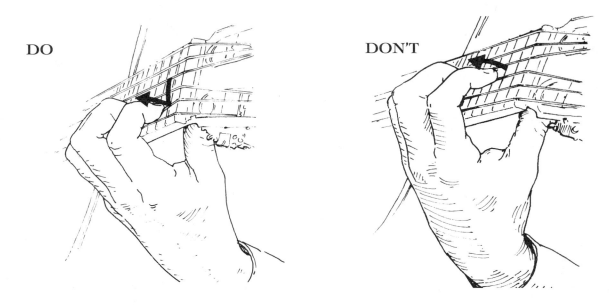

DO   **DON'T**

In the first example, the finger pulls down into the fingerboard and next string. At first casual glance, it appears as if the finger may indeed be pulling itself off the string; but in reality, we are making the string snap-off of the fingertip. This, of course, causes the finger to pull into the next string, creating a sort of left-hand rest stroke. Use this adjacent string to help our finger empty out, and to spring it back into a ready position above the string.

The second illustration shows a pull-off done habitually by many people. Practically taking the term "pull-off" literally, the finger is pulled upward away from the string and fingerboard, thus creating a consistently feeble tone.

Practice the following slur exercise with these things in mind:

From a state of dynamic relaxation (meaning, in this case, the finger is pressing down just enough to make the note sound), move, or snap, the finger quickly through the string, then spring it back up with a relaxed gesture. Both the snap and the spring are one motion. The finger should not seem to be forced back up. Rather, it is quickly brought back up with the springboard of the string to help you.

Repeat this on each string.

Repeat each example at least 4x.

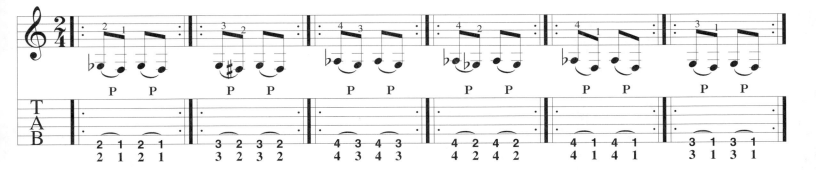

Finger Independence

It is crucial that the fingers be able to maneuver independently of one another. The following exercises are designed to increase both vertical and horizontal dexterity. Some are also incorporated into the *Daily Warm-Up Routine* on page 56 of this book.

#1

Put down or "fix" the fingers indicated on the third string. Play the notes indicated with the free finger. It always helps me to think of the fixed fingers as being rooted to the very back of the neck, and the free finger as being as light as a feather. I also prefer practicing these in the fifth position, where the frets are closer together and the horizontal reach is easier and therefore less fatiguing over an extended period of time.

#2

Now we will deal with moving two fingers and fixing two fingers. The same principles apply here: rooting the two fixed fingers through to the back of the neck, while keeping the two movable fingers as light as possible. You'll find there's more potential for strain here, so take it slow and focus on the stretch as you extend your fingers, and then on the opposing motion as they pass each other. Finally, sustain the second bass-note as your next finger travels up to the treble, and then hold the second treble-note as you switch to the bass, etc.

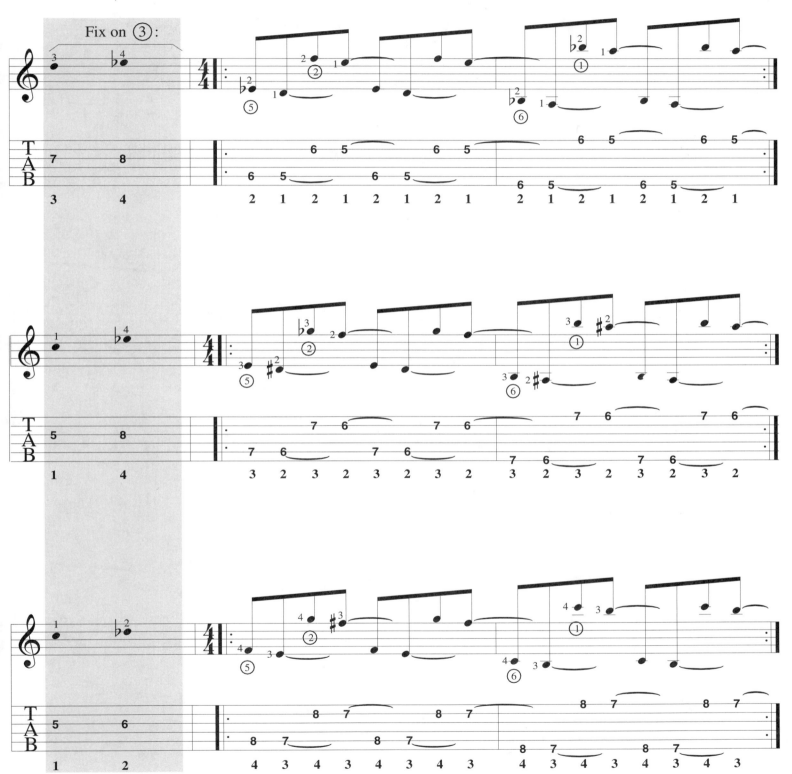

continued on next page

#3 - Opposing Motion

You should practice this exercise two ways:

First, play each one *staccato*, with all the notes detached. Let the fingers of your left hand feel the spring upward between fingering changes. Remember not to spring upward any higher than one inch. After your fingers release the notes, instantly place them right above the next two notes. Take your time and play through each variation this way.

The next step is to play them as *legato* as possible, without a noticeable gap between the notes. To do this, stay on the strings until the last possible instant. Visualize your fingers going to the next two notes, then switch.

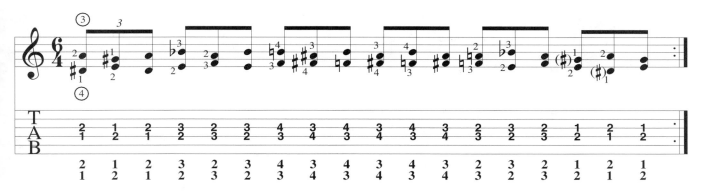

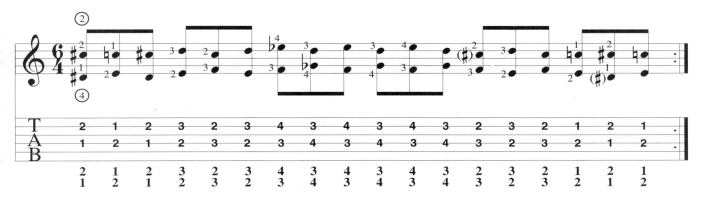

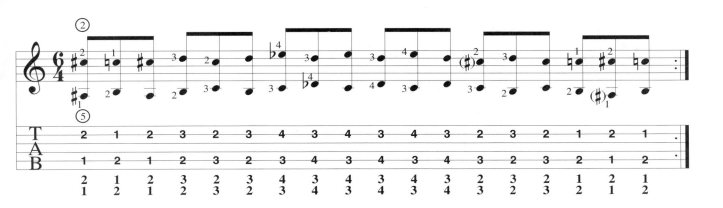

continued on next page

(#3 - Opposing Motion, continued)

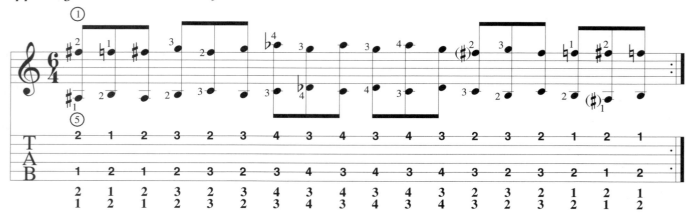

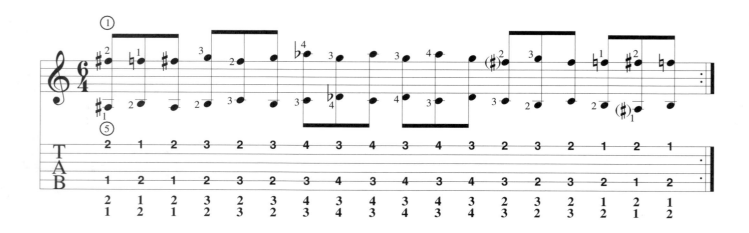

#4- Horizontal Character Builders

It's exercises such as this one that earned this book its title. We're focusing on several things during this next set. First of all, because they're slurs we have to make sure we play them cleanly and with the proper snap. Try to make each one sound clearly. Relaxing or emptying out each finger when it lifts up is very important. Since you're extending your finger across the strings at practically the same moment you're lifting it, there is less time to empty it. This is why I insist that you begin slowly. Start with a metronome setting of ♪ = 60!

We also need to concentrate on extending the fingers. Try to position each finger over its next note right away. Play slowly, but move quickly.

IMPORTANT: If you feel any pain in your hand, wrist, or forearm, stop and rest! Of course, try to distinguish between pain and a little fatigue. The whole point of these exercises is to strengthen your hand, increase stamina and work certain muscles that may not have been worked before. Your hand will be a little tired after each exercise, and this is normal. Pain, however, is not normal, and the only way to get rid of it is to stop playing.

I also suggest you rest for five minutes or more between each exercise until the fatigued feeling goes away. Then you can start again. Either go on to the next one or repeat the one you've just done. If you feel that a particular stretch is impossible for you, skip it. You'll be able to do it in time.

Begin at ♪ = 60

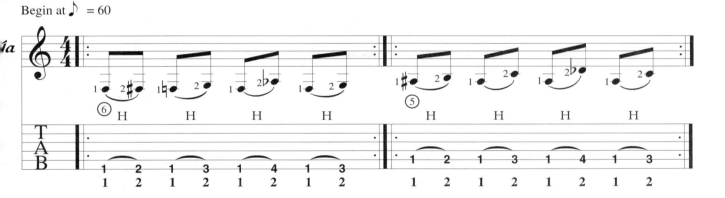

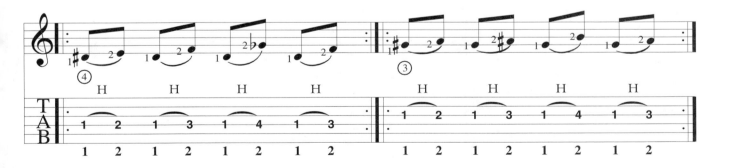

continued on next page

continued on next page

#5 - Odair's Favorite Drill

I'm not really certain that this is his *favorite*, but I did borrow it from Odair Assad and his brother Sergio when they suggested that a student practice this a lot during one of their master classes. It's self-explanatory. Just make sure you hold down the notes where indicated.

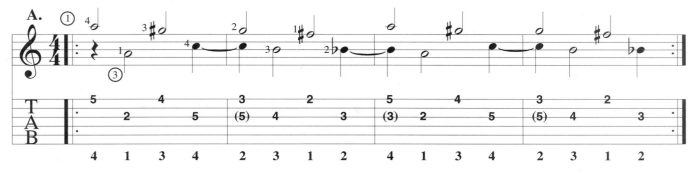

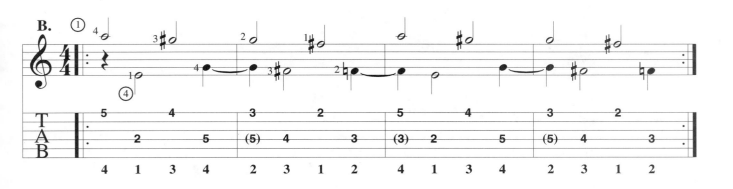

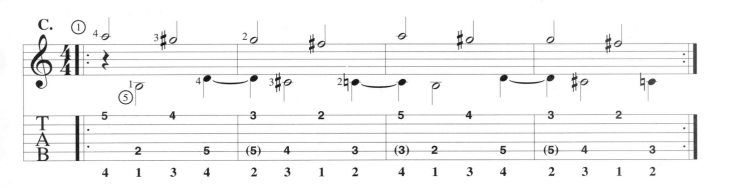

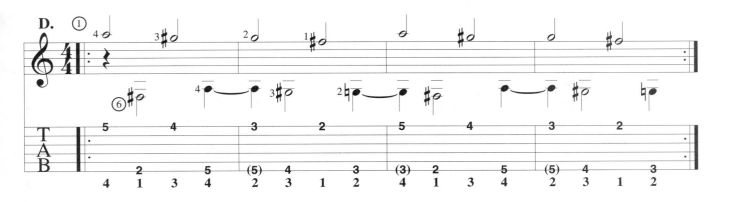

#6 - "The Spider"

Here's a fun one. It's called "the spider" because, when it is played smoothly, your hand resembles a spider crawling up the neck. Isn't that marvelous?! Great at parties. Thrill your kids.

As you lift one pair of fingers, instantly get them into position above the next pair of notes.

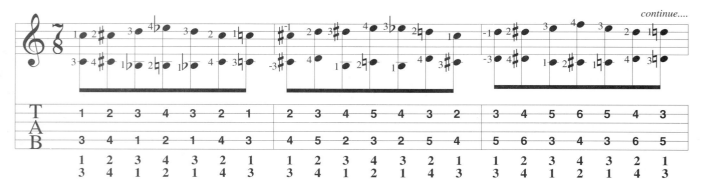

continue....

The Barre

Playing lots of barres is always annoying. However, that tired, burning feeling you get between your thumb and first finger is probably just the result of pressing too hard. Also, if you stop to think about it, only rarely does a barre require the entire finger pressed against the fingerboard.

Weight vs. Pressure

First, analyze your barre. Are you allowing the weight of your arm and gravity to assist you? Look at the picture on the right and see how your weight should be channeled.

Notice how the angle of the neck, the angle of the forearm, together with the gravity that is pulling on the elbow are combining to naturally channel the weight back into the fingerboard. Believe me, it is much easier to feel it for yourself than trying to put it into words.

See page 4 to review how barres are notated.

Being Selective

The other element you need in solving your barre problem is selectivity. Figure out exactly which notes underneath your finger need to sound. You rarely need every millimeter of your finger squeezing all the time.

Usually you'll find that what makes your finger most uncomfortable is having to straighten it out completely, or applying pressure to the middle joint. Look at this next chord, and play it on your guitar. As you play it, are you clamping your entire finger across all six strings? You shouldn't be. What notes from this chord really need to be played with your first finger?

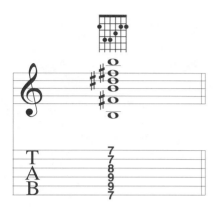

Answer: the low B on the sixth string, the F♯ on the second, and the B on the first. Just three notes! So in this case you don't have to lock your middle joint. In fact, you can relax it, thus creating a barre that makes your finger look curved.

Now here's a good one for you!

Lightly barre the seventh fret. Play each note written by applying pressure only to the appropriate part of your finger. Sometimes you'll find the string coinciding with a crease in your finger. If this happens, gently roll or move your finger slightly until the note sounds clearly. Since everyone's fingers are different, we all have to experiment for ourselves.

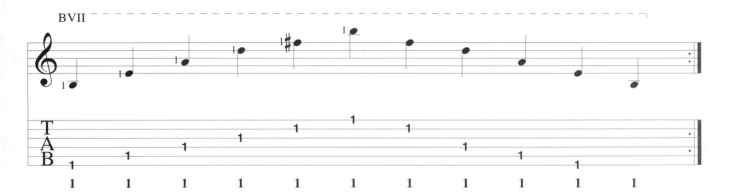

Summing It All Up

It seems to me that the main cause of many peoples' hand problems and pain is the retention of tension. They hold the tension in their fingers and hand while they shift, change notes, or any other time they are not actually playing a note. There is no reason for this aside from technical insecurity. Know what you're hand is doing at all times, which fingers are pressing and which are not—be totally aware. This is the first and most important step towards a secure technique. What you do or don't do in between the notes means everything.

Quadrivial Quandary by Andrew York— A Four-Voice Study for the Left Hand

Here's an exquisite little chord study that Andy has written for the left hand. There are just a few things to keep in mind while working on it:

1. Take your time—a slow tempo and quick, accurate movements are the key.
2. Always visualize the next chord in your mind's eye before moving there.
3. Observe all held notes.
4. Although the ideal tempo is ♩ = 80, begin much slower and without a metronome. A metronome would force you to stay with the beat and move to the next chord whether you are ready or not.

Quadrivial Quandary

Andrew York

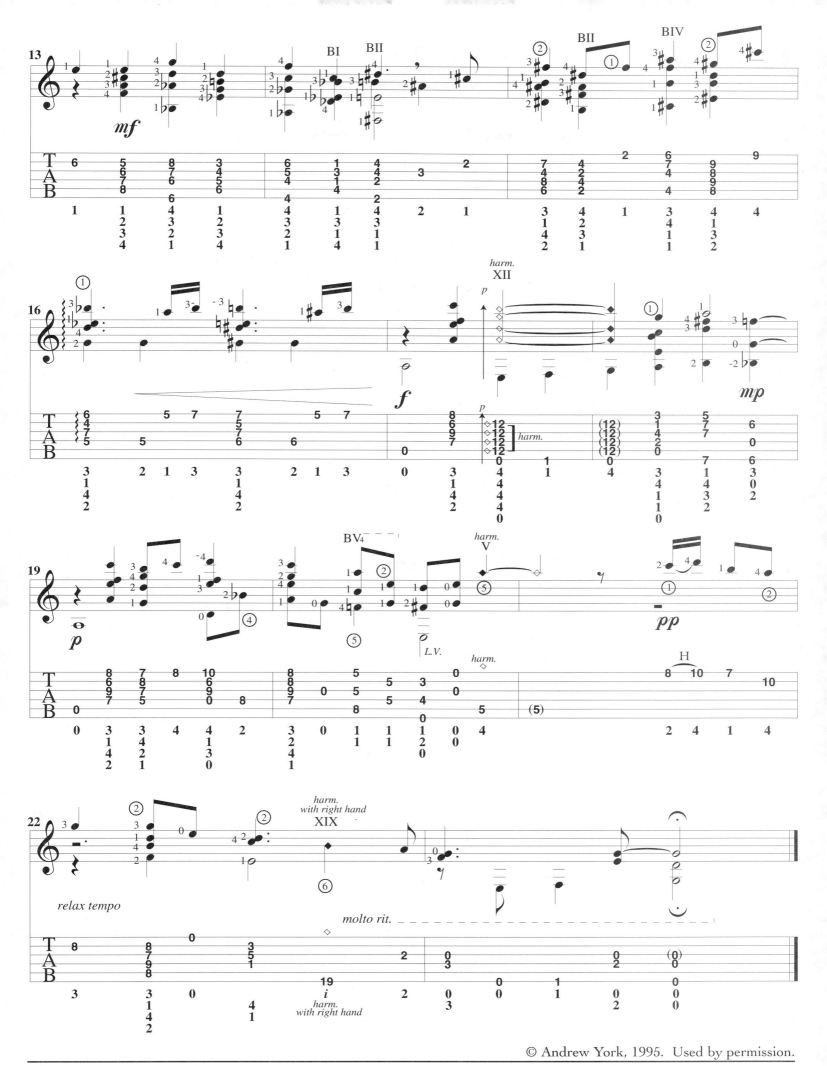

Fanfare by Brian Head
A Slur Study

Brian's *Fanfare* is not only a great slur work-out, it's appropriate for a concert program, too. Technically, it contains a good balance of slurs and opposing motions. Focus on the following:

1. Practice slowly and execute all slurs accurately with a good, solid tone.
2. Make sure that all held notes are sustained during any other slur activity.
3. Take note of the meter changes.

Fanfare

Brian Head

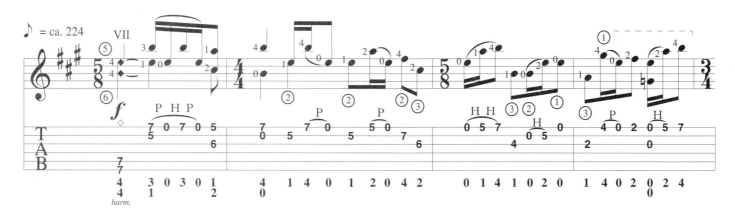

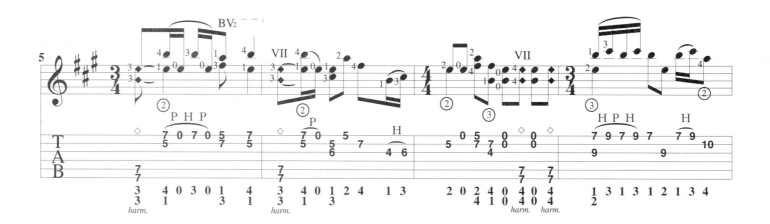

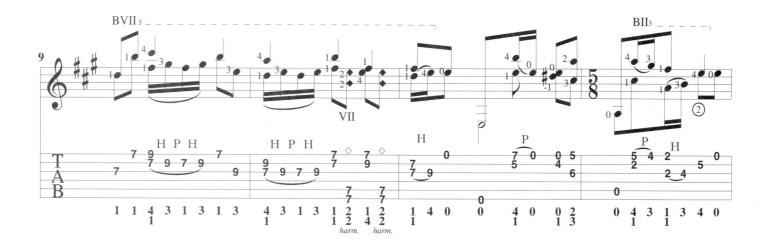

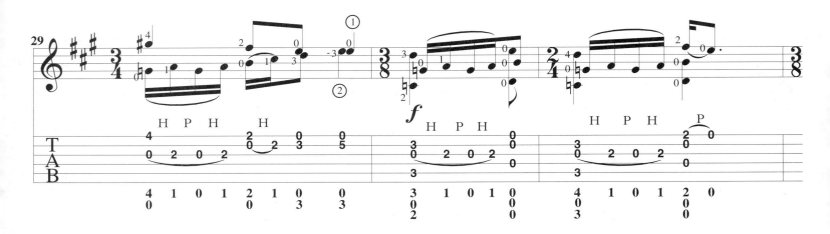

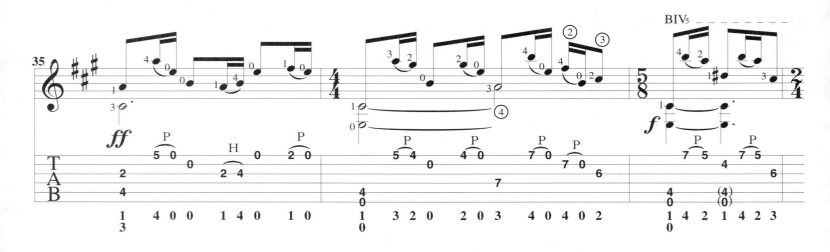

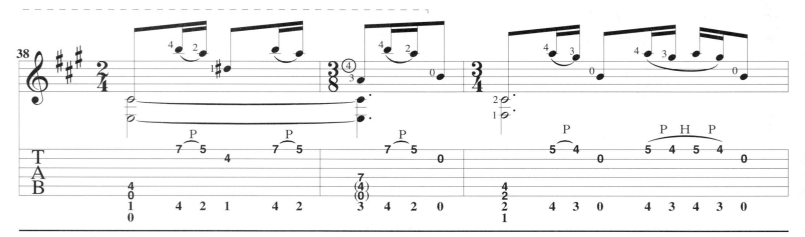

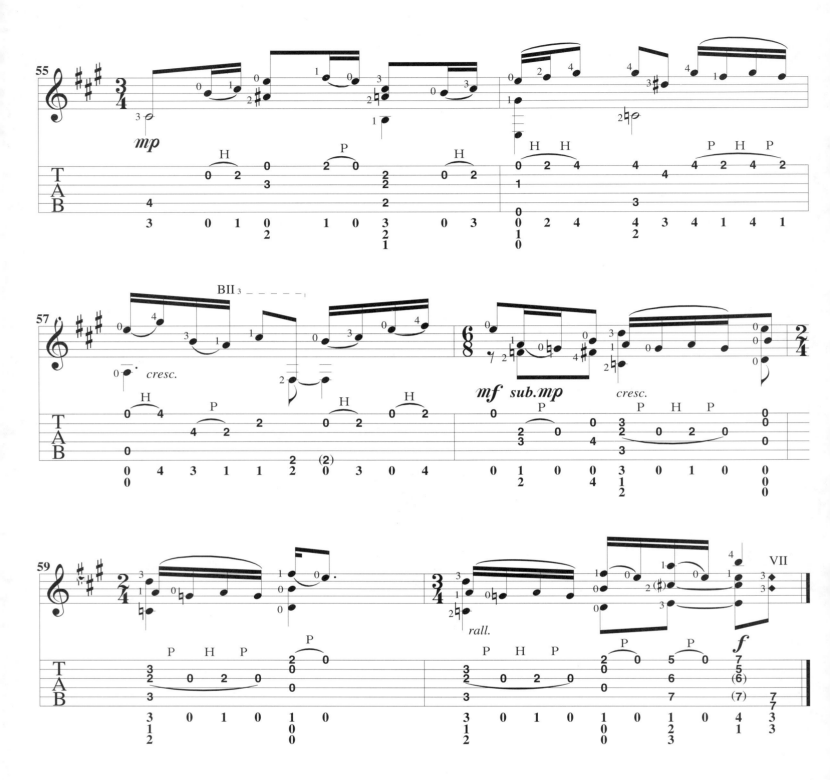

© Brian Head, 1995. Used by permission.

"To climb steep hills requires slow pace at first."

• William Shakespeare •

The Right Hand

Tone Production

The right hand produces sound. Although the quality of tone is determined by both hands, the type of tone and the volume are controlled primarily by the right hand.

There are seven ingredients that go into tone production:

1. Nail length and shape.
2. Choice of stroke: free stroke or rest stroke.
3. Hand position and the angle of the fingers to the strings.
4. How the fingertip and nail approach the string.
5. How the fingertip and nail prepare on the string.
6. Finger pressure against the string.
7. The release of the fingertip and nail from the string.

Each of these ingredients influences all the others. One will generally determine what comes next. For instance, your choice of rest stroke or free stroke will determine your hand position, and therefore the angle of the finger to the string. This will then determine how the finger approaches the string, and thus how the finger is finally prepared on the string. All of these contribute to the security of the fingers on the string and your ability to apply the appropriate pressure; and the pressure inevitably effects how the string will be released. The length and shape of the fingernail effects how successfully you will be able to carry out all of the various parts of the stroke.

Nail Length and Shape

If a nail is too long, the speed and ease with which the fingertip and nail go through the string is considerably diminished. This is because the resistance has been increased. A bad nail shape can also create undesirable resistance against the string and cause some very interesting but unsavory sounds.

The reason we play with our fingernails at all is to assist us in securing and controlling the string, to enhance our volume and tone. So it is important that you grow and shape them in a way that will make it easier to play and sound good.

The following illustrations show some different nail types and ways to shape them. You'll also see how to gauge their length.

Nail Length

To gauge the length of your nail, hold your finger out horizontally and then place a file against the fingertip at a right angle. If the nail and flesh touch the file at about the same time, the length is good. If you have to tilt the file forward or back the nail is either too long or too short.

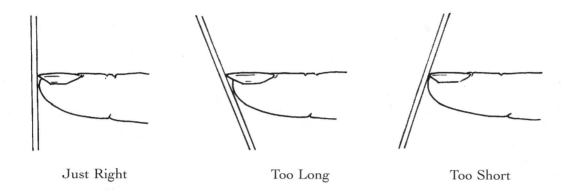

| Just Right | Too Long | Too Short |

Nail Types

These nail types represent the four basic shapes: curved (Type A), flat (Type B), hooked downward (Type C) and bent upward (Type D). While the curved shape is ideal, the latter three shapes are the most common.

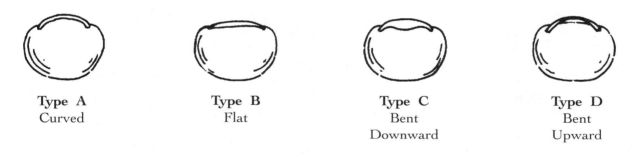

Type A
Curved

Type B
Flat

Type C
Bent
Downward

Type D
Bent
Upward

Here are the basic "do's and don'ts" for shaping the nails:

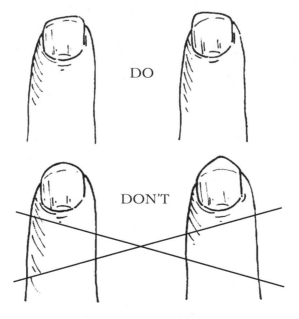

DO

DON'T

There are various reasons why a nail shape will be either advantageous or not. One of the most important issues is how the string moves across the nail. Shapes #1 and #2 to the right (the "don'ts" from the bottom of page 35) cause the string to travel "uphill" with too much resistance. These shapes also prevent us from using enough of the nail, since they release near the middle of the nail.

Either of the two shapes (#3 and #4) shown on the right allow the string to travel along a "ramp" and release from the nail more easily, at the same time using the maximum amount of nail possible. Your nail type will determine which of these two shapes is best for you, but they both enable the string to travel along desireable ramps.

The old advice that we should file our nails to match the contour of their fingertips just doesn't always work. Although it may not look all that bad to you, what the string "sees" from its angle is a hill that has to be climbed. Sometimes if it is rounded too much, as in shape #2, a point develops, creating even greater resistance and a more abrupt release point. This is absolutely devastating if your nail is a Type C, or "hooked" nail. With shapes #1 or #2, the hook is exaggerated instead of minimized.

Nail shapes #3 and #4 are both good, but have different effects. Shape #3 is most common and advantageous, as it aids in pushing the string into the soundboard during a stroke. This generally results in a fuller sound. Because the ramp is angled upwards, this shape can result in much more resistance (nail to string) than shape #4. As you can see, shape #4 is angled slightly downwards, making the string travel downhill during a stroke. This allows for a very fast, smooth release; so fast, in fact, it makes some players feel that their finger is slipping off the string. Many players who use rest stroke primarily, and who play at less of an angle to the string, prefer this shape, while those who prefer using free stroke favor the #3.

If you have had a problem finding a good shape to match your nail type, the following page contains some matches you may find useful.

Nail Type	Shape

A

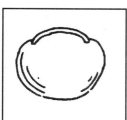

#3 **#4**

 or

B

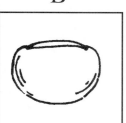

#3 **#4**

 *or*

C

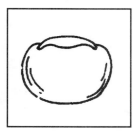

#3

D

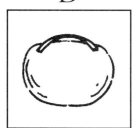

#3 **#4**

 or

preferable

Shaping the Nails

Always use a file, as opposed to a nail cutter, to shape the fingernails of your right hand. Nail cutters leave the fibers of your nails with jagged ends, even if you polish with sandpaper afterwards.

Always file your nails with your fingertips facing you. Position the file underneath the nail at a slight angle and look down the surface of the file. This gives you the ideal view of the edge of the nail. Try to create a straight line as seen from this angle, as illustrated on the right.

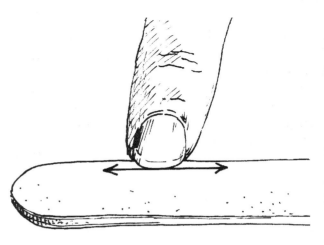

Ideally, the file will touch the edge of the nail evenly across its width, and fit securely underneath it without rocking around. If the shape of your nail is too round, you will notice a rocking motion as the file moves around the nail's edge.

The line illustrated to the right will only be seen from this particular angle. The nail shape is not actually straight or flat. It will still appear rounded, although possibly not as round as the fleshy fingertip.

These ideas for shaping your nails are only suggestions. There are many variations on the four nail types discussed in this book. While I have found that the corresponding shapes suggested here work well consistently, experimentation is encouraged. Find out what works and feels best for you.

Angle and Placement

In order to achieve a full, or "fat" tone, we must give special attention to the angle of the fingertips to the strings. Note that when the fingers are initially placed on the strings, only the flesh makes contact. The nail makes its contact when pressure is applied. The illustration below shows an advantageous angle.

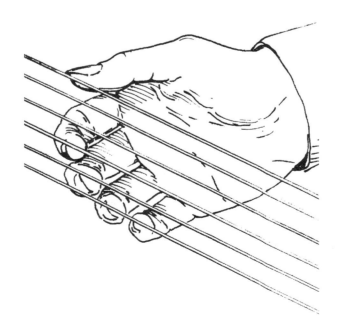

When a finger moves straight back into the palm from this angle, it is actually moving over a healthy portion of the string surface (as the string uses the nail as a "ramp") which enhances the tone. This angle, however, creates a scraping sound on the wound bass strings, and should therefore be adjusted to a straighter angle for playing on the fourth, fifth and sixth strings.

Rest Stroke (Apoyando)

What a rest stroke really does is set the string vibrating more in the direction of the soundboard. Physically, this results in more resonance inside the guitar and on the soundboard itself. This is why a rest stroke is generally perceived to be fuller sounding than a free stroke.

Position

The large joint, which is where the main thrust of the stroke originates, is placed over the next lower adjacent string. For instance, if you are playing the first string, the large joint should hover above the second or third.

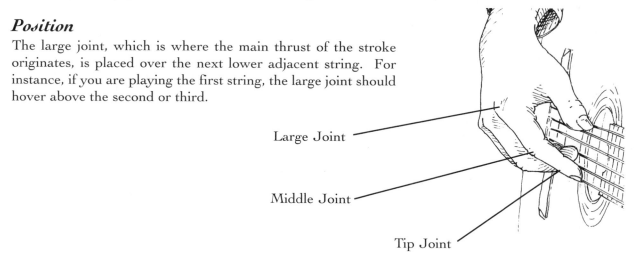

Large Joint

Middle Joint

Tip Joint

The Movement

Although all of the joints in the finger move, the joint that actually moves the finger is the large joint (the metacarpo-phalangeal). This is the source of the thrust that pushes the finger through the string. It's also the only joint that moves the finger in towards the hand, allowing for a big round sound. The others move the fingertip upward, which, if we restricted the movement at the large joint, would cause a thin sound. Think of it as similar to legs walking: we propel ourselves forward from our hip, not our knees or ankles.

Although they all take place in such rapid succession that they blend themselves together into one movement, there are three steps involved in every stroke:

1. Planting (preparation)
2. Pressure
3. Release

Planting

Planting simply involves preparing, or placing, a fingertip on a string accurately enough to execute a stroke (see the illustration above). It also helps to briefly stop the vibration of a string between notes — just enough to control the tone. Slapping the finger down onto a vibrating string causes a slapping sound, and, more often than not, the nail alone makes careless string contact creating a sizzling effect. By planting we control where we land and minimize any unpleasant noises.

Planting the fingers is also the only effective way to control articulation. Those who claim they never plant their fingers, and in fact actually teach their students not to plant, maintain that planting a finger stops the sound, which is undesirable. This, of course, is true when the preparation is exaggerated, as we do when we are first learning how it is done. But planting gets much more advanced than that. Anyone who makes a good sound, who can control their tone and articulation, and has any kind of developed awareness of what their fingers are doing, is planting their fingers to some extent.

Pressure

The pressure we put on a string displaces it to some degree. The distance we move a string in one direction determines how far it will go in the other direction. This establishes how loud a note will be. No matter what amount of pressure you put on a string, always make sure you feel the string move underneath your finger. Be aware!

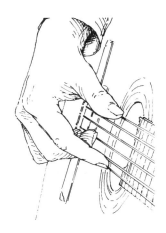

Release

The release is what determines the sound. In the case of a rest stroke, the finger simply uses the pressure it has applied to pull through the string, emptying out as it comes in contact with the adjacent string. Emptying the finger aids in springing it back into place for the next note. Notice how a well-executed rest stroke goes in towards the soundboard.

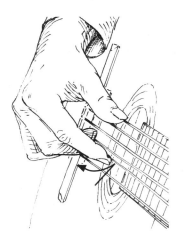

Free Stroke (Tirando)

A free stroke is essentially the same as a rest stroke in that the setup and movement are similar. One could justifiably describe a rest stroke as an interrupted free stroke, or a free stroke as a rest stroke with follow-through.

There are two important things to strive for during a free stroke:
1. Set the string vibrating into the soundboard as much as possible.
2. The finger should follow-through straight back toward the heel of the hand.

These elements help optimize the potential for a full sound. A well-executed free stroke can be just as strong as a rest stroke.

The drawings below show a good free stroke. Notice that the large joint is positioned above the string it is playing (as opposed to being over the next lower string, as in rest stroke). This allows for optimum string displacement and a good follow-through. If this joint is back any further than this, the probability of the smaller joints pulling upwards more to bypass the next string increases. Avoid this and keep the main thrust coming from the large joint.

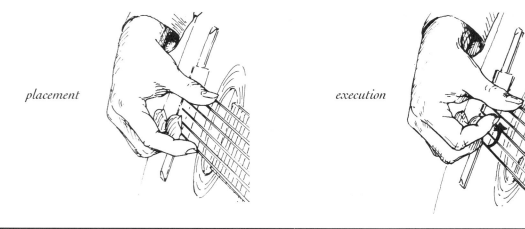

placement   execution

Right-Hand Finger Independence

Walking

Great as a daily warmup, or when used as technical practice, the following "walking" exercise is simple yet effective. It is probably one of the most effective exercises in this book. After realizing that the main obstacle keeping me from progressing in my scales was crossing strings, I started "walking." I practiced only crossing strings—and it worked! I still practice this every day, and my scales now feel secure. In fact, when I do hit a snag, I'll work on the right-hand string crossing all by itself (see Problem Solving in Scales on page 90).

Here are the things you should keep in mind:

1. Do the exercise using rest stroke and free stroke. Rest stroke is the more challenging of the two.
2. As soon as you release one note, place your finger on the next string *immediately*.
3. Always strive to produce a good, solid tone.

If you focus on these three things, you'll get results. Make sure you practice with one finger at first, then alternating two (or even three) fingers. I would suggest spending the first few practice sessions working on the one-finger drills. Focusing intensely for 5 to 15 minutes should be good enough. Spend longer if you wish, but concentrate. Then, move on to the *i, m* alternation. I mainly stick with *i* and *m* because that's how I finger most of my scales; but by all means, make up your own patterns, especially if you like playing your scales with three fingers instead of two.

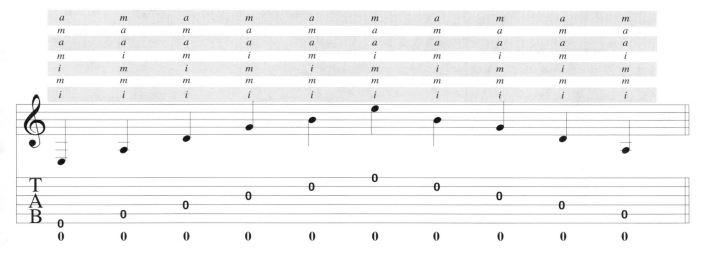

Variations:

Also, try playing the first note rest-stroke, the next one free-stroke, the next rest-stroke, and so on. In addition, practicing your scales with just one finger is great!

Arpeggios from Tarrega's
The Complete Technical Studies

These are great exercises for developing your finger independence. They involve standard finger combinations in the context of awkward string crossings.

Practice using free stroke, with a full sound. Wherever string crossing is involved, make sure you prepare the next note immediately after releasing the last.

If you are one of the multitude of players who have difficulty playing a thumb rest stroke while doing free strokes with your fingers, this is a good opportunity to work on that technique.

Take your time. It is best to work on a few of these during a practice session, and become comfortable with them before moving on. You don't necessarily have to play them all every day.

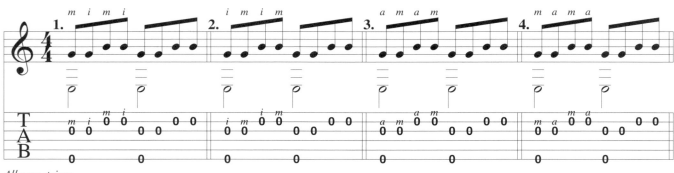

All open strings

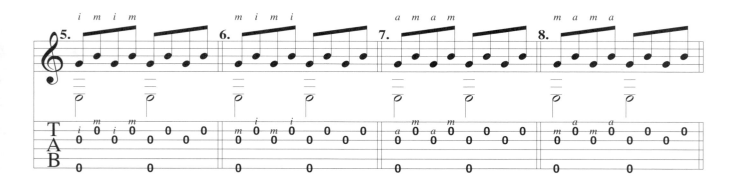

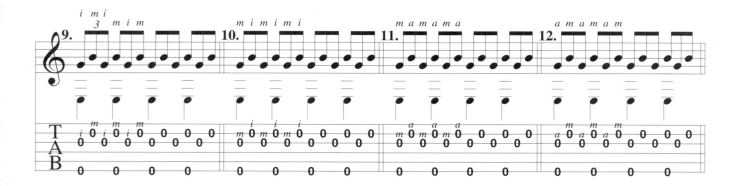

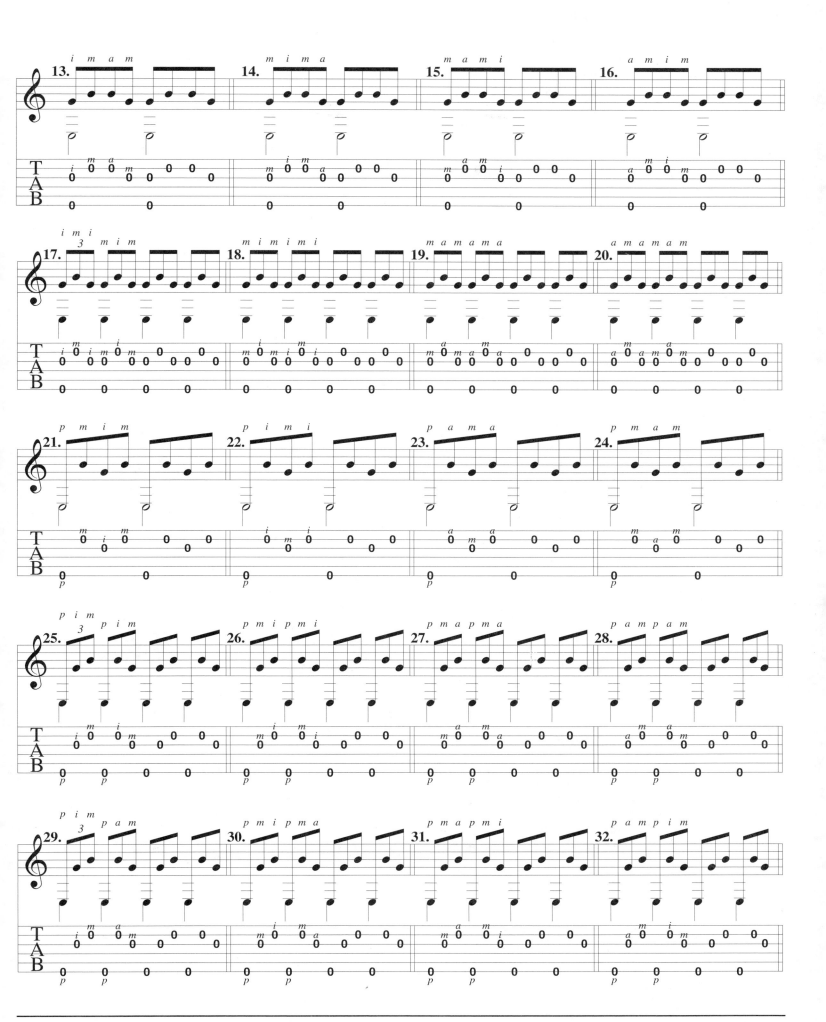

The Thumb

Just as the fingers move from the large joint, the thumb moves primarily from the wrist joint. The tip joint moves to aid in the follow-through, or to help produce a desired tone or effect.

The thumb also moves the string in toward the soundboard before releasing.

NOTE: For a free stroke, the string is displaced downward, and the thumb releases low, close to the soundboard.

COMMON MISTAKE: The thumb displaces the string parallel to the top, and releases high.

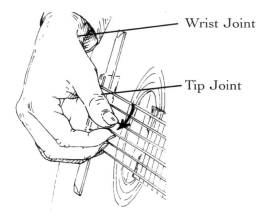

Wrist Joint

Tip Joint

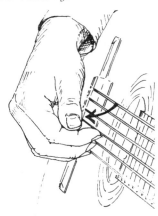

Shaping the Nail

The shape of your thumbnail should allow the thumb to play the string easily, without catching.

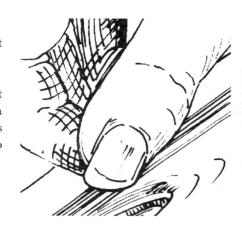

The illustration below shows a good shape. It won't catch on the string; in fact, it almost fits evenly against the string. However, a more rounded fingertip will require less of a slant, while a more tapered fingertip may require more. This thumbnail shape also allows for greater control of tone colors, since it makes it easy to switch from an "all-nail" tone to an "all-flesh" tone, or play with the standard "flesh/nail" combination.

Develop That Thumb!

Many players tend to sentence the thumb to confinement in the bass. The logical association of the thumb with the bass aside, there really is no reason to forgo the development of this prized appendage! Most of our thumbs are weak and lacking in agility. It's time to let them out for some air and exercise! Also, we should explore some less ordinary uses for the thumb.

The thumb is the most awkward of our manual protrudences—that's true. But strengthening this finger can only help the other parts of your hand. A balanced hand is a happy hand.

Most of us have trouble executing consistantly good thumb rest strokes. At first, try playing this next exercise entirely with *p* rest stroke. Then try playing just the first note of each triplet with rest stroke, and the third (after the slur) with free stroke. Controlling the alternation of rest and free strokes is not only a basic technical skill, but it is something you will use over and over again in your musical interpretations.

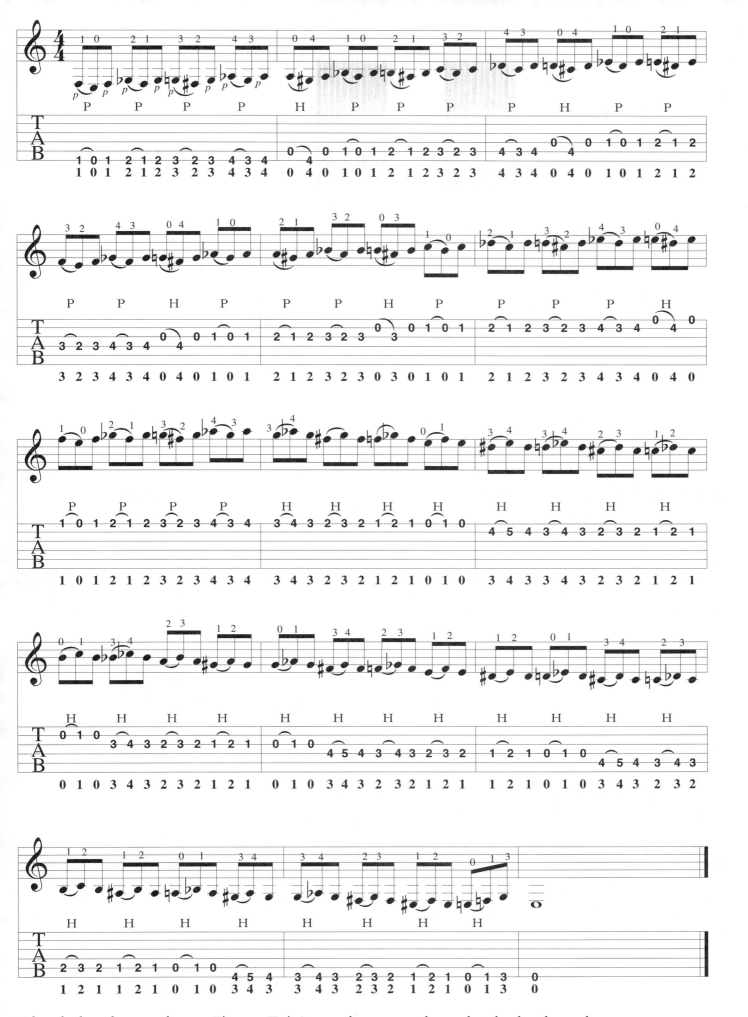

Take a look at the next chapter, *Flamenco Techniques*, to learn more about what the thumb can do.

Flamenco Techniques

What Else Can the Thumb Do?

Flamenco! Included in the bottomless bag of tricks of flamenco guitarists is the way they use their thumbs. Far from trickery, though, the thumb is used mostly out of necessity. The guitarist must be heard through all the singing, hand-clapping, and the piercing footwork that is flamenco. Many fast passages that we classical guitarists would play with our fingers are easily done with the thumb by the flamenco guitarist.

Although not always directly applicable to the classical repertoire, practicing some of the techniques will expand our capabilities. As an example, here is a falsetta from a *Soleares* that was taught to me years ago by the incredible Juan Serrano. This is the exact right hand fingering he used—practically all thumb. All thumb strokes are played rest stroke. And YES!, it is possible!

SOLEARES FALSETA

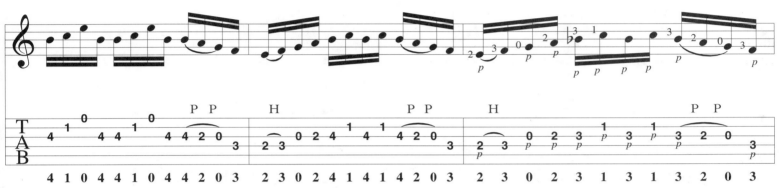

Alzapua

Alzapua is a technique which utilizes the back of the nail, as well. It comes from the Spanish word *alzar*, meaning *to lift*. It is a powerful technique, and does wonders for strengthening the thumb.

The arrows pointing down indicate that the thumb goes down (towards the floor) through the strings. The arrows pointing up indicate that the thumb moves upwards (towards the ceiling) through the strings. The key is to move the thumb quickly, trying to sound all the notes simultaneously. If you can hear separations between the notes, you're moving through the strings too slowly. All single notes must be played with thumb rest strokes.

ALZAPUA FALSETA

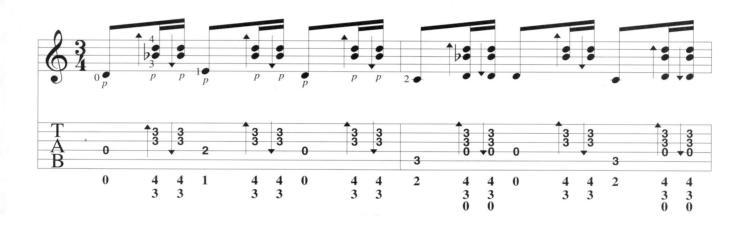

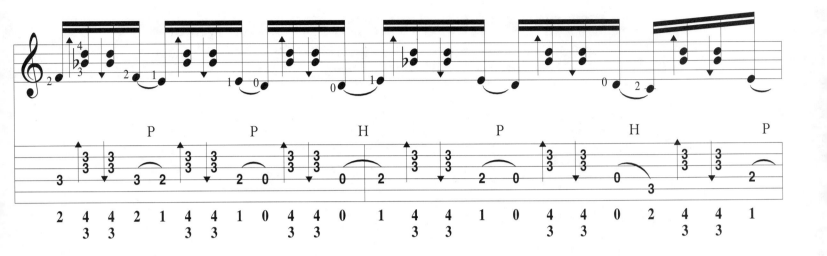

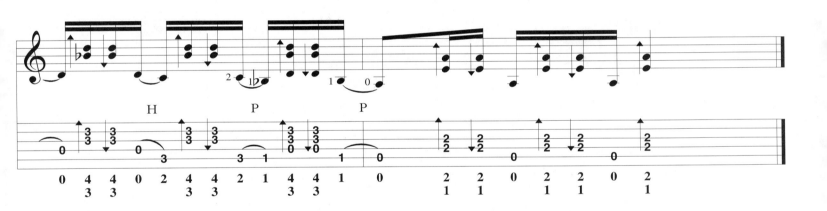

Rasgueados

This is another flamenco technique which is sadly neglected by many classical guitarists. A *rasguaedo* is really more of a percussive effect than a strum. It is done by hitting the strings with the backs of the nails.

Practicing rasgueados develops the extensor muscles, which are the muscles that move the fingers outward, away from the palm. Many players believe that playing scales with considerable speed and accuracy is dependent upon how quickly we can move our fingers out, not in. This would certainly explain why most flamenco guitarists have the ability to play blazingly fast scales.

For now, practice your rasgueados by anchoring your thumb on the fourth string as you play on the first, second and third strings. It is helpful to begin by alternating only two fingers. Play the examples on the next page with the indicated alternation combinations.

Attack the strings from just above ...

... not like this.

On page 51 there are some rasgueado patterns that include all of the fingers. Some are traditional patterns, and some are a little out of the ordinary.

The letter *"c"* indicates the little finger (the pinky, *chiquito* in Spanish). For all the examples except numbers 3 and 6, keep the fingers extended until they have all finished playing.

Examples 8 through 12 involve an exchange between the thumb and the fingers (either all together or individually). This requires a particular motion of the wrist. The wrist should remain as straight as possible while pivoting, as if turning a doorknob. As the thumb plays its upstroke, the fingers follow it into a ready position. As the fingers play the downstroke(s), the thumb follows them into a ready position. In Examples 10 through 12, the thumb returns to a ready position only after *i* has played.

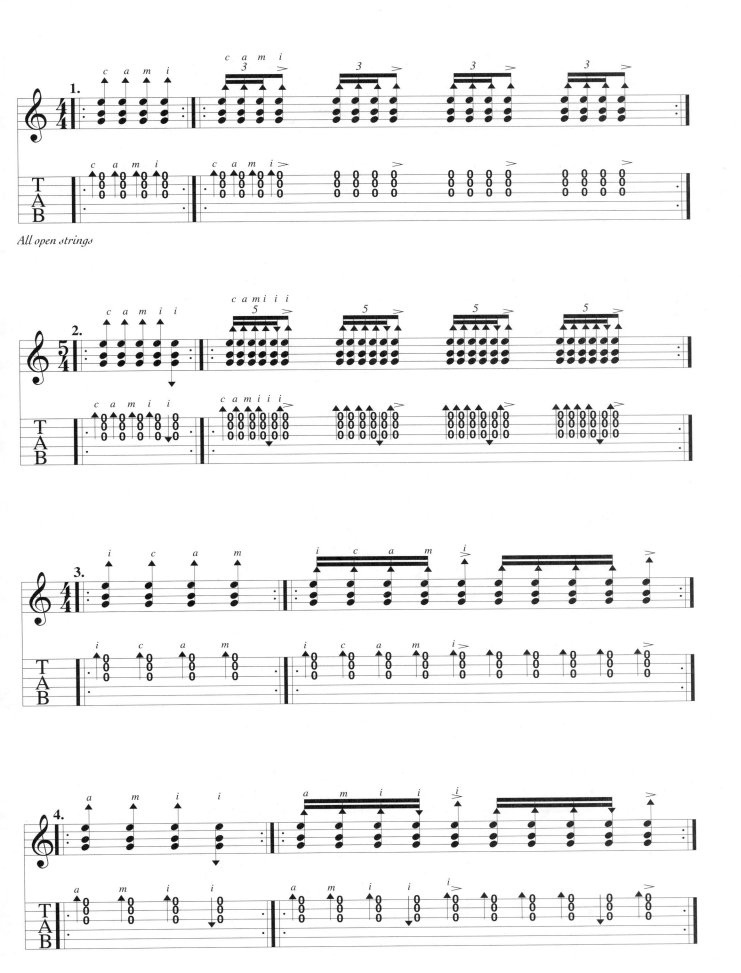

All open strings

continued on next page

(Rasgueados continued)

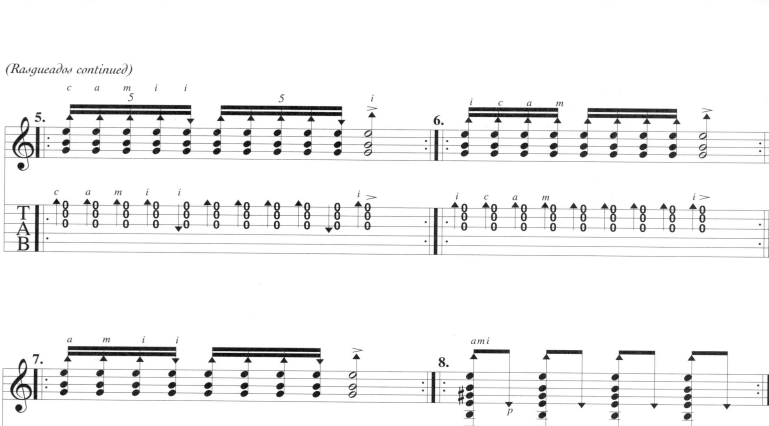

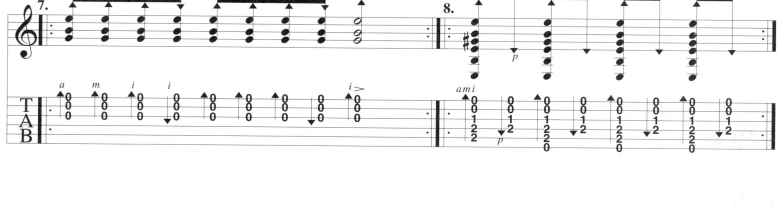

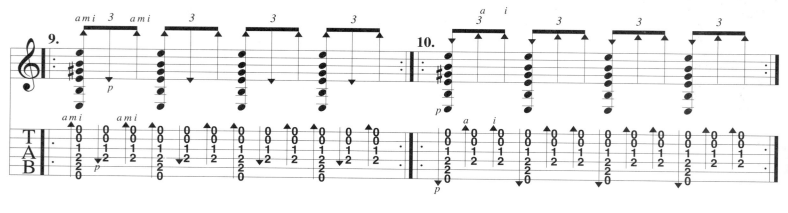

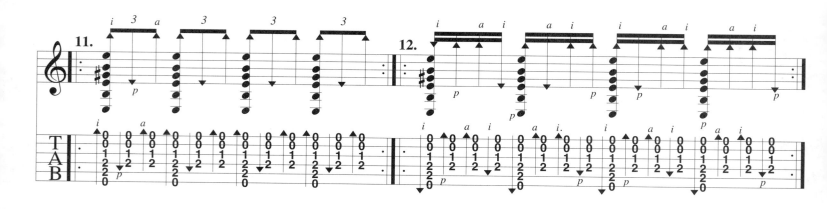

Some Practical Applications

The weight and textures that good rasgueados add to one's playing are substantial. The Spanish repertoire particularly benefits from it. I have included just a few excerpts from Turina and Rodrigo where some alternate right hand patterns are particularly beneficial. But please be aware that these are solutions that work well for myself, and as your skills become sharper, so will your own problem-solving capabilities.

from Turina's *Sevillana*

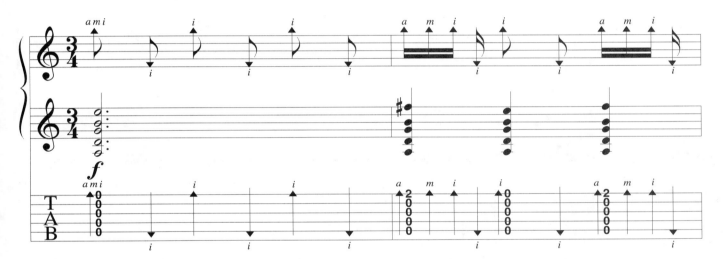

from Turina's *Ráfaga*

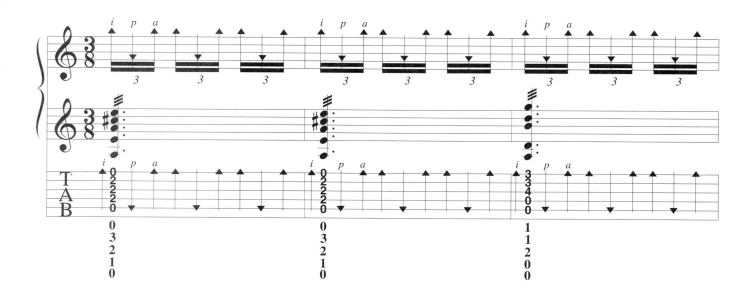

Or, if you want to emphasize the chord changes:

↑ = a downward strum with a finger.

⇡ = a downward strum with the thumb with emphasis.

from Rodrigo's *Concerto de Aranjuez,* 2ND MOVEMENT

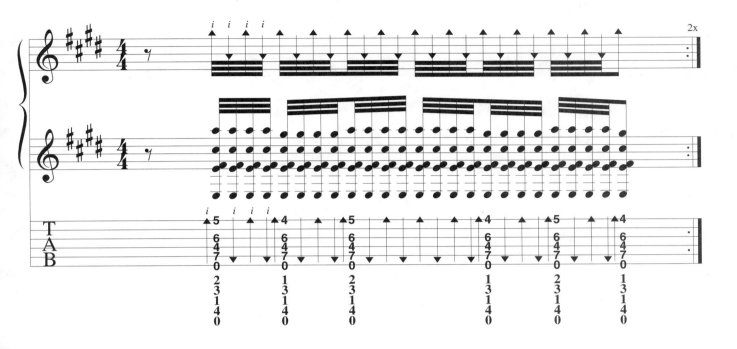

Or:

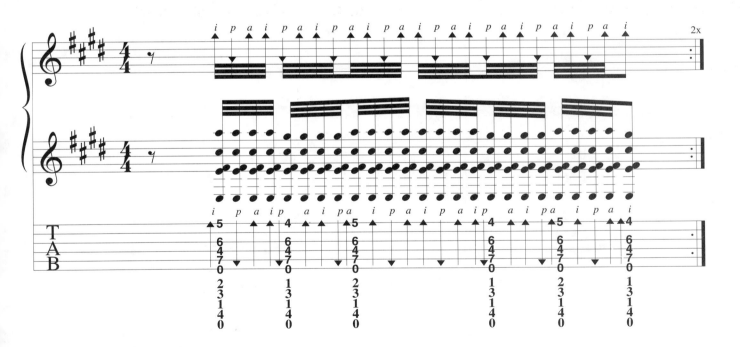

Daily Warm-Up Routine

The following exercises have been compiled to form an effective daily technical routine. I would suggest going through the whole thing initially, and noticing where your particular weaknesses lie. You can then isolate those exercises that will strengthen them. On the other hand, I find going through the entire set to be a great warmup.

Left-Hand Walking—#1, #2 & #3

GOALS:
1. Remember the basic left-hand position.
2. Keep right-hand fingering simple and keep the focus on the left hand.
3. Avoid playing with the pads of the fingers or right on the fingertips (refer to the hand position illustration on page 9).
4. Strive for consistent accuracy rather than speed.
5. Move quickly between notes, avoiding gaps in the sound.

#1

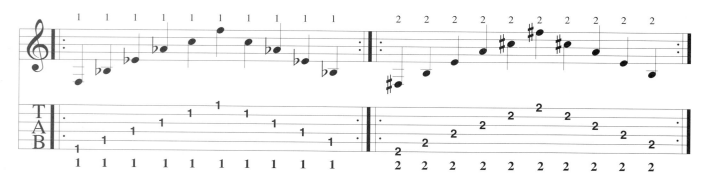

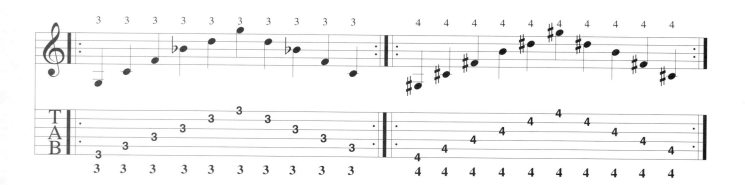

#2

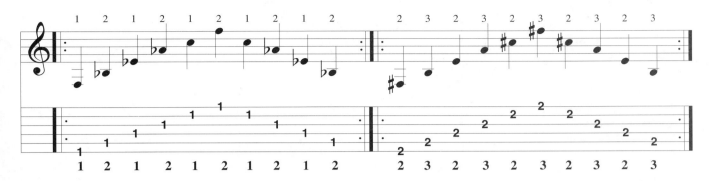

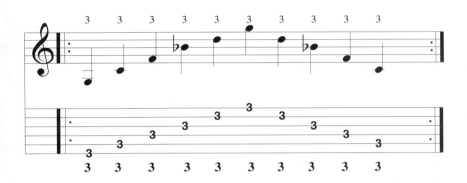

#3

Here are some rhythmic variations to apply to #1 and #2.

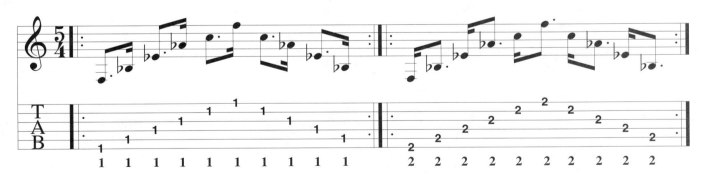

GOALS:
1. Move the fingers quickly rather than from a great distance.
2. *Empty* (see page 11) a finger after it has played, then shift weight to the next one, and so on.

#4

Descending Slurs—#5

GOALS:
1. Start from a *ready position* where both fingers are on the string, but not pressing.
2. Pull off quickly into the fingerboard, "snapping" the string off the fingertip.

#5

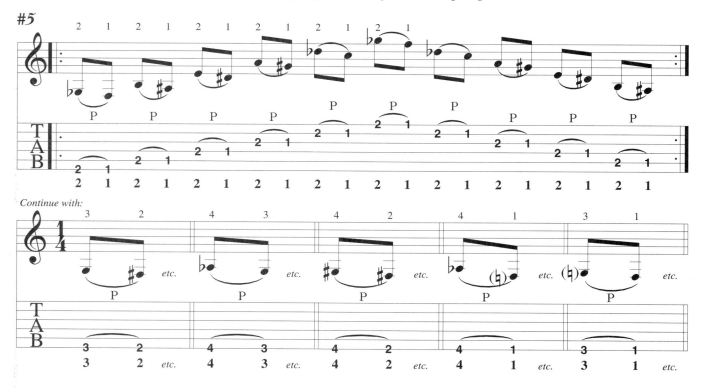

Triplets—#6

These are important. In fact, if you only have time for one left-hand exercise, *do this one*!

#6

Fixed-Finger Exercises—#7 & #8

GOALS:

1. Anchor the fixed fingers into the fingerboard with weight (try not to press).
2. Keep the moving fingers light like feathers.
3. While exchanging fingers 3 and 4, it's alright to pivot slightly, but otherwise only move the fingers themselves.

#7

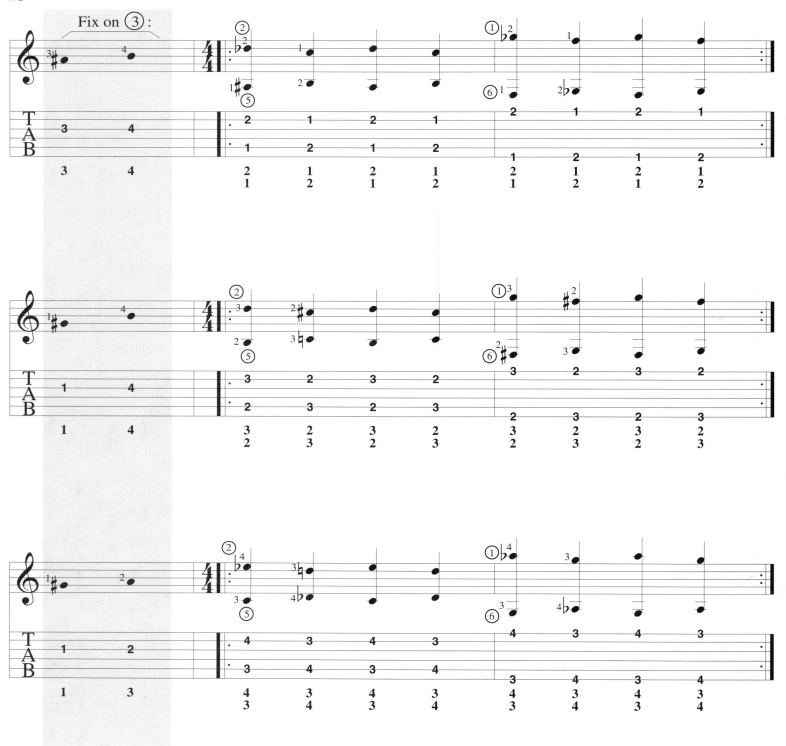

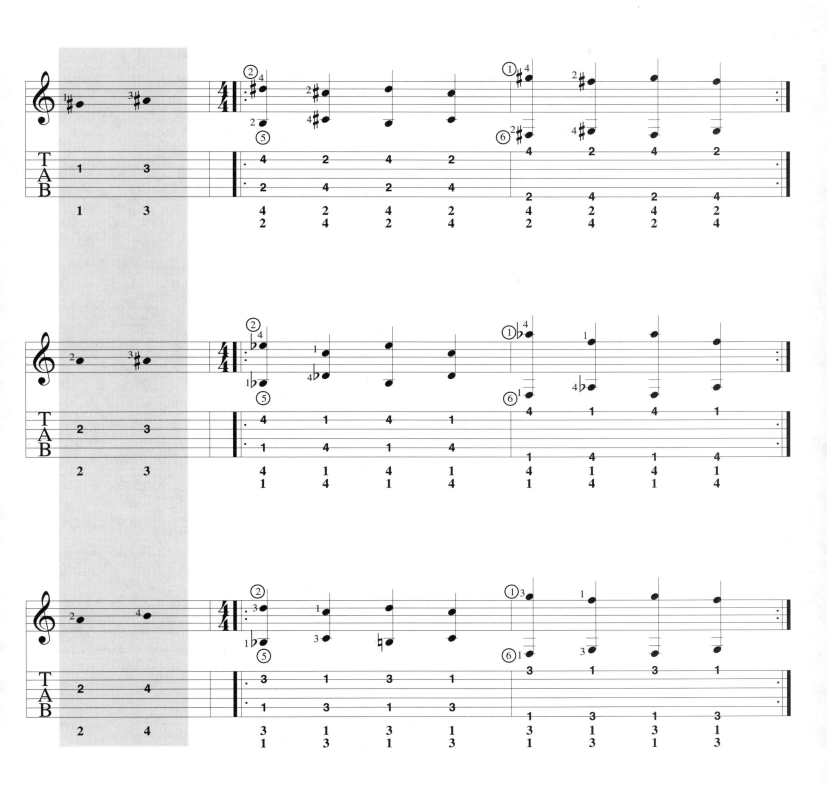

Right-Hand Walking—#9

GOALS:

1. For warming up, use rest strokes.
2. "Bounce" back immediately to the next note.
3. Project (dig in and get a good volume!).
4. *Always* strive for good tone.
5. Making up your own versions or variations to suit your own needs is encouraged!

#9

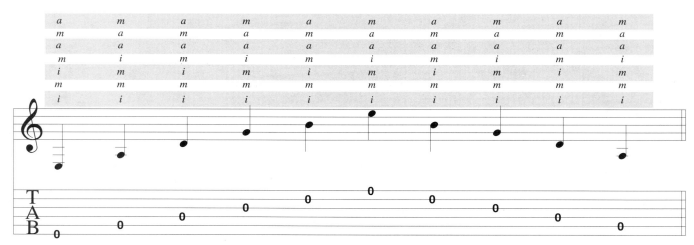

All open strings

Some rhythmic variations:

GOALS:

1. Anchor the right thumb on the fourth string.
2. Attack the strings from slightly above using the backs of the fingernails.
3. Sound all three strings at once by snapping quickly through the strings, rather than strumming.

#10

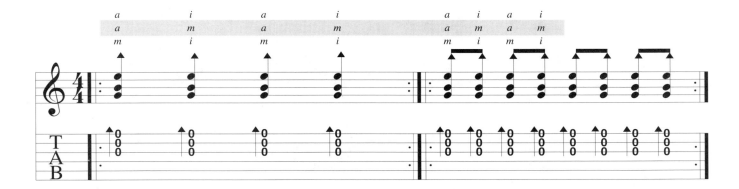

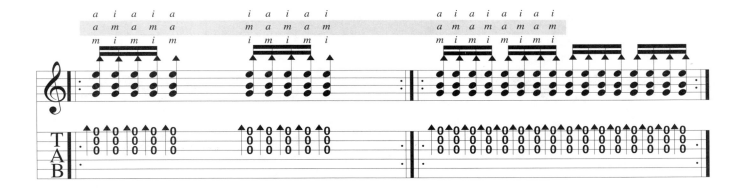

"DO or DO NOT; there is no TRY."

• Yoda •

Tremolo

Judging from the frustrated attitudes I have encountered on the subject, tremolo is certainly one of the most challenging of techniques. Difficult and frustrating it may be, but I believe we are fortunate as guitarists to call it our own. It isn't tremolo that is unique to our instrument, but the way we do it. It is an illusion we create—an illusion in which the melody seems to be constantly sustained, although it is not.

The key to success in playing a good tremolo is not speed, as most students believe, but evenness of articulation. The more articulate each note, the faster the tremolo seems. The more articulate the tremolo, the more control we have over it.

Psychological Outlook

Strive for control rather than speed. Learn to think of your thumb as just another finger. One of the problems many players have with tremolo is that they think of their thumb as a heavier, more forceful appendage. This leaves them with the psychological burden of *fitting in* the other three notes between thumb strokes. Instead of dividing tremolo into *one + three* notes (thumb plus the three fingers), these individuals should think of it as simply *four* notes played by four consecutive fingers.

Let's try to put this into practice. Before you play Exercise #1, just play steady eighth notes on one string, using, of course, *p-a-m-i*. Play them at a slow tempo. Listen very carefully to make sure they sound even - are they all the same volume and of the same length? This is an important preliminary exercise for tremolo, because eventually you will rely on your ears to play your tremolo for you; you will hear an inaccuracy, and your fingers will automatically adjust. Get used to listening well instead of just watching your fingers.

Exercises

Exercises 1 - 3

Keep the notes short throughout your tremolo practice, not just in this exercise. I have found that practicing a slower tremolo staccato makes it sound extremely smooth when played quickly. It also feels easier to play quickly after having practiced it in this way slowly.

In this exercise we are gradually incorporating *speed bursts*. When doing speed bursts of any kind, it is essential that one always returns immediately to the slower note values. This gives us a reference point; and, eventually—when the length of the burst increases—the faster version should feel no different than the slow one. Playing all the notes staccato for now enables us to hear the length and volume of each note more clearly, and as long as we can hear it, we can control it.

GOALS:
1. Practice each one until the fast notes feel easy.
2. Do not move on until the first one feels easy.
3. Strive for equal volume on all notes.
4. Strive for equal duration on all notes.
5. *Feel* each note *before* you play it.
6. *Listen* to each *as* you play it!

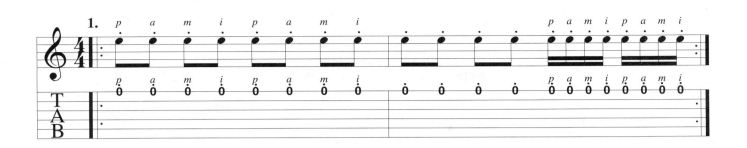

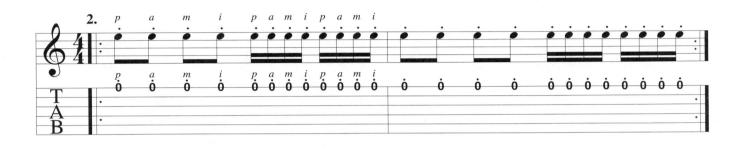

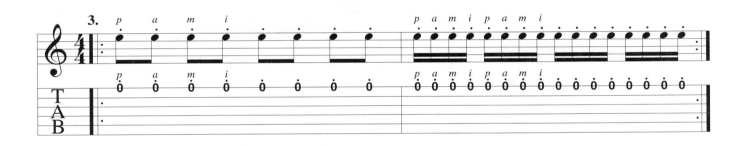

Exercise 4

This exercise involves moving the thumb from string to string. It is very important to gain control of the thumb. Place it accurately and make direct movements. You may want to incorporate the idea of alternating slower notes with faster bursts in this exercise. Don't ignore the thumb tone!

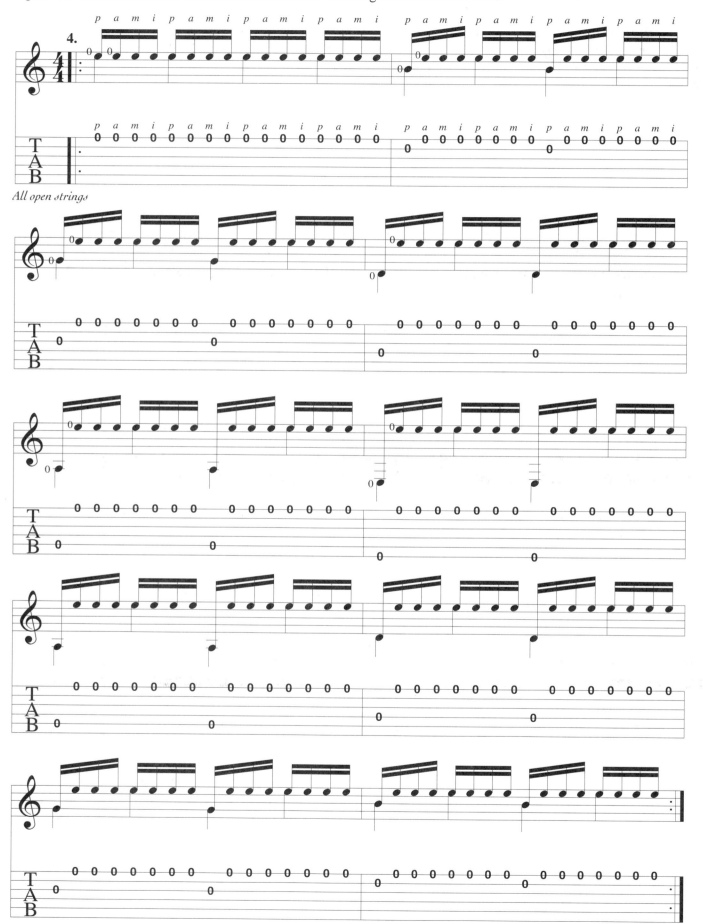

All open strings

Exercises 5 - 10

Here are some different ways to practice tremolo. Each one accomplishes something slightly different.

Adding accents is beneficial for an uneven tremolo; just listen to yourself and pinpoint what note is weaker than the others, and accent that note. The accent is not put there to make the note louder, necessarily, but to insure that you **feel** that note more intensely. Accenting it without feeling the note is empty practice.

Numbers 8 and 9 are two different types of tremolo used by flamenco guitarists, and each should be mastered.

Number 10 is my favorite overall remedy for a sloppy, weak, or uneven tremolo: a backwards tremolo. Try it!

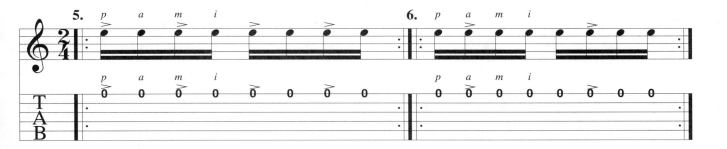

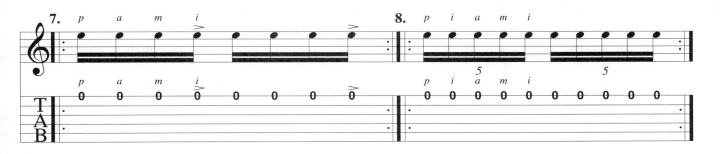

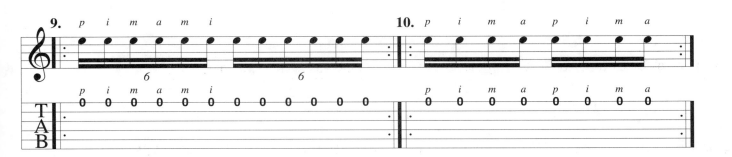

Exercise 11

Learning to change the tremolo pattern as illustrated in Exercise 11 is a very useful tool for getting control over this technique. This kind of practice is especially useful when applied to an actual piece of music, such as *Recuerdos de la Alhambra, Campanas del Alba*, or whatever tremolo piece you are currently trying to smooth out.

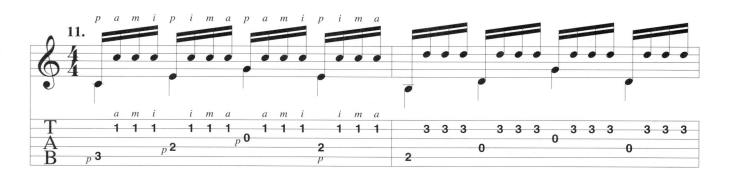

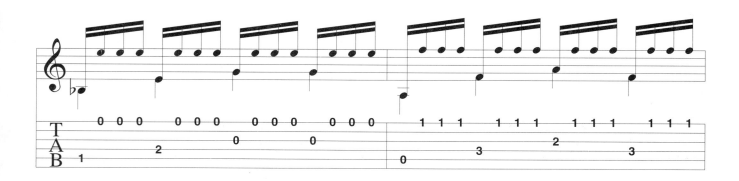

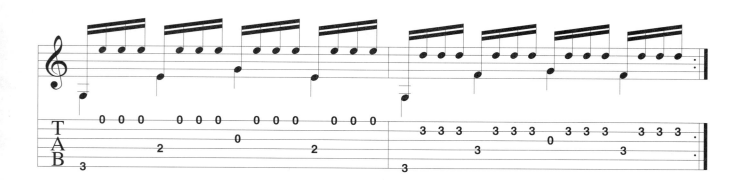

Lopsided Tremolos

The examples that follow are certainly good for anyone to practice, but are primarily designed to help correct "lopsided" tremolos. A lopsided tremolo is one that has too much of a gap between either *p* and *a*, or between *i* and *p*.

If your tremolo sounds like this...   *Practice this:*

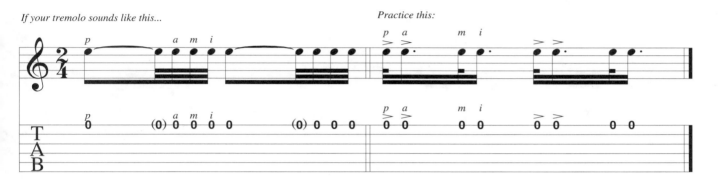

If your tremolo sounds like this...   *Practice this:*

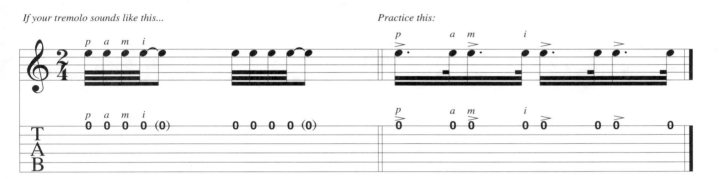

Chant by Brian Head: A Tremolo Study

This piece is directly inspired by the composer's orchestral composition of the same name. It is unique in that the notes often change in the middle of the tremolo, thus creating a constantly fluid line. Take note of the following:

1. Make sure the moving notes within the tremolo are well synchronized.
2. Even though the ideal tempo is ♩ = 132, start as slow as 60 or so while learning the piece.
3. Strive for clarity rather than speed. A well-defined tremolo and a slightly slower tempo (if necessary) will best enhance the dark mood of the piece.

Chant

Brian Head

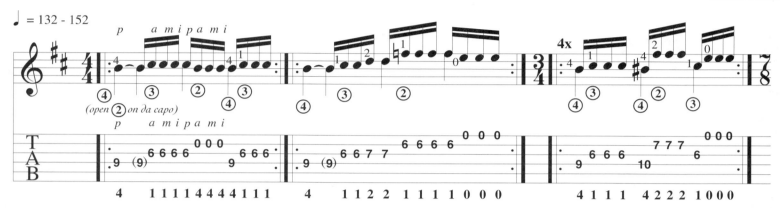

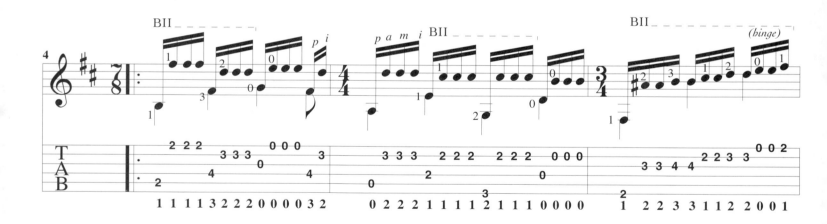

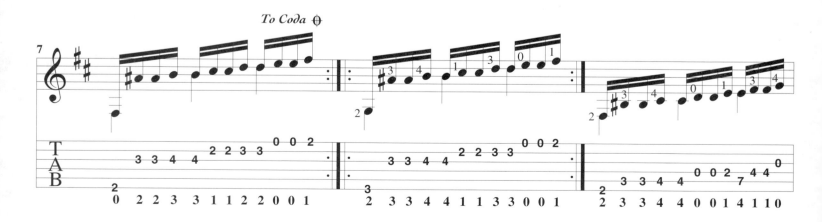

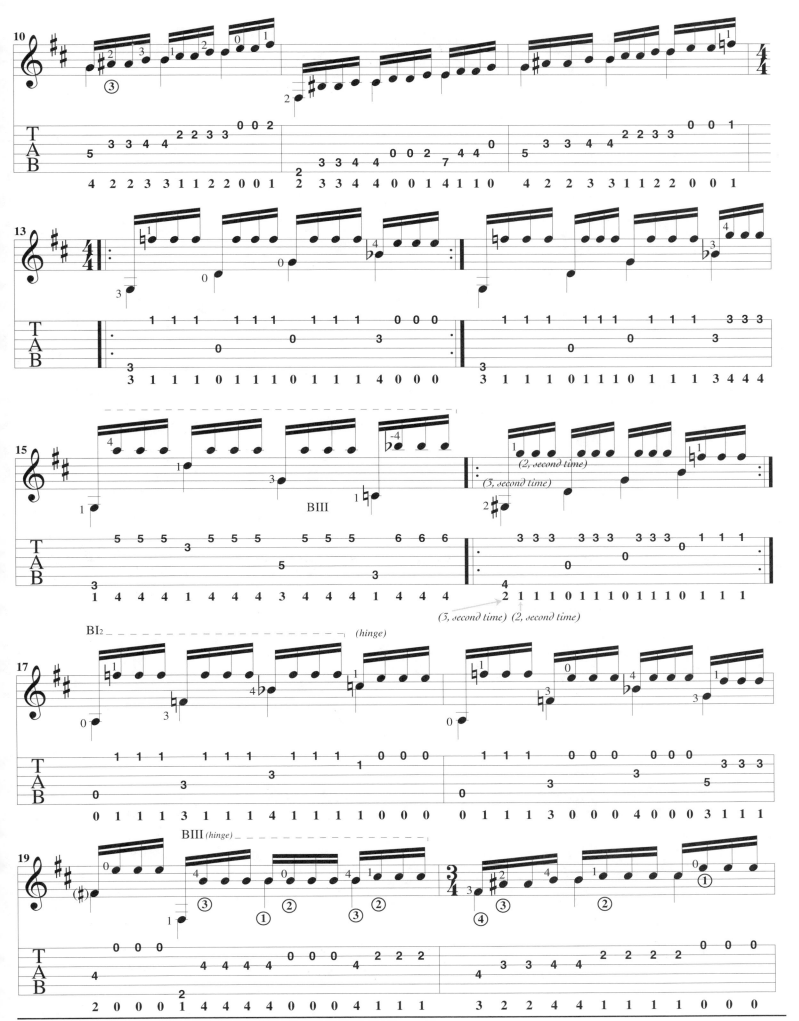

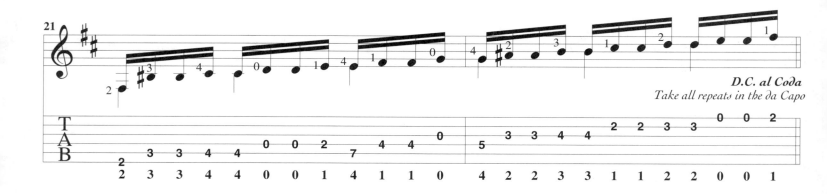

D.C. al Coda
Take all repeats in the da Capo

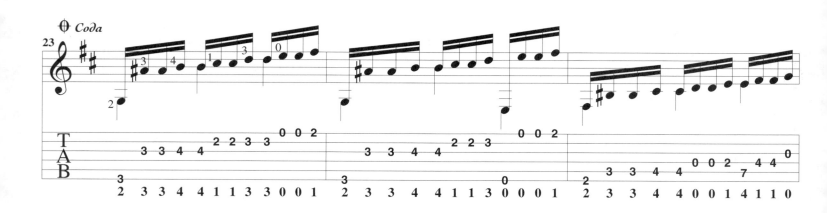

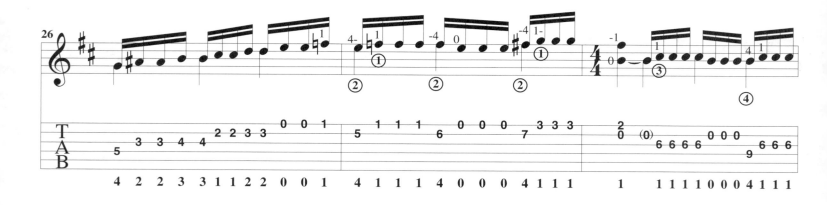

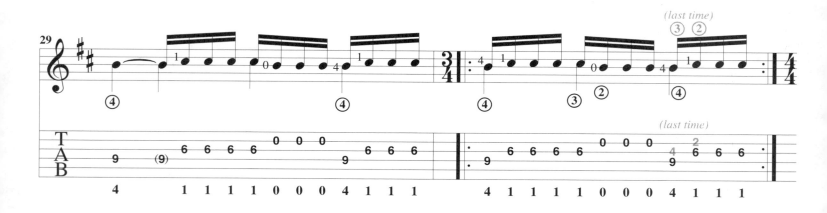

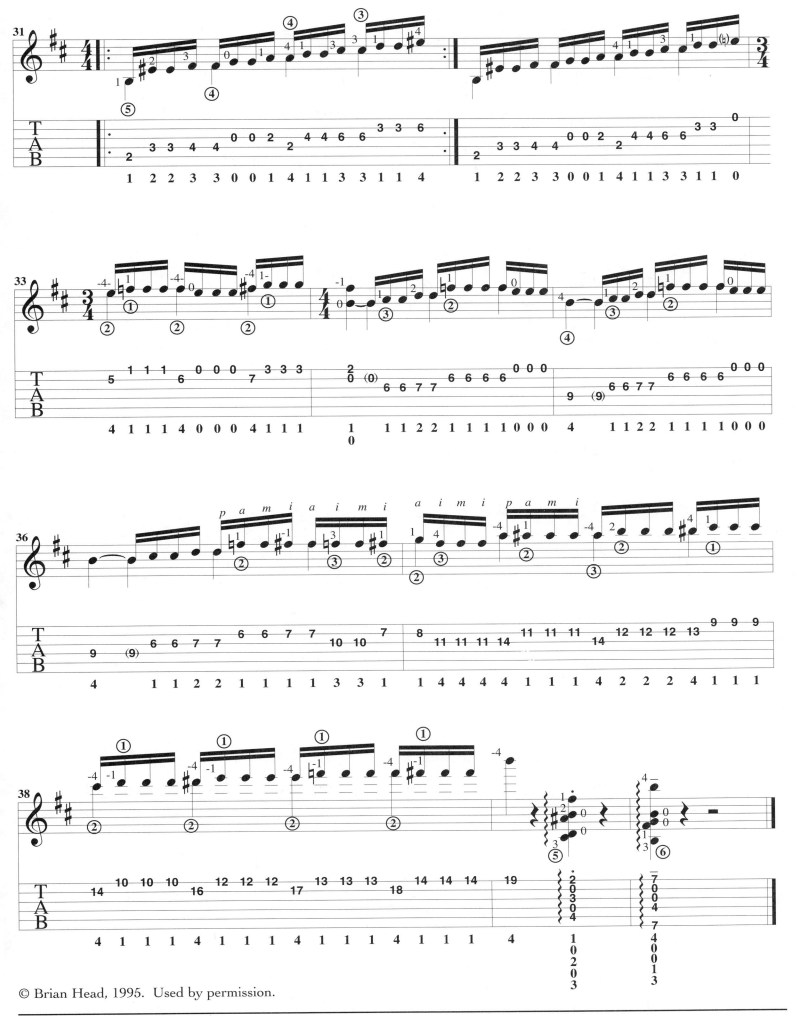

© Brian Head, 1995. Used by permission.

Scales: Control and Velocity

Control is more important than speed. If you can exercise control while playing, speed, when necessary, will follow easily. There are several general misconceptions about speed, especially in scales:

Misconceptions about speed...

1. *Without a certain amount of speed one is not a good player.* The fastest players are not necessarily the best players.
2. *Speed is a goal—rather than a tool.* Speed is something we use towards a musical end.
3. *One must be able to play very fast for long stretches of time.* Many students fail to recognize that the vast majority of scale passages in the repertoire requiring speed are only one or two measures long.

There are four elements to be mastered for the development of scale speed. They are:

1. Right-hand velocity.
2. Synchronization of the right and left hands.
3. String - crossing.
4. Piecing together.

Each element shall be addressed briefly, along with an exercise.

Right-Hand Velocity

Right-hand velocity refers to how well you're able to pluck a series of notes in rapid succession with your right hand. Towards this end, practice *speed bursts*. A *speed burst* is a long string of slow notes interrupted by a short burst of fast notes. At first, you should frequently return to the slow notes between bursts; the slower notes act as a launching pad for the quick ones.

Here are a series of speed-burst exercises. Make sure each exercise is secure before moving on to the next one. While they're new to you, practice them using rest stroke, being strict about the staccato markings. After that feels good, try playing them using a legato free stroke.

1.

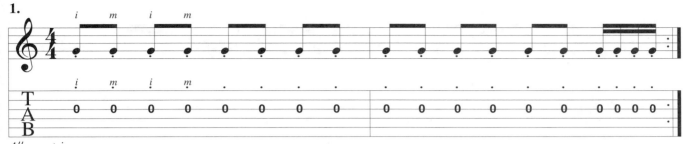

All open strings

2.

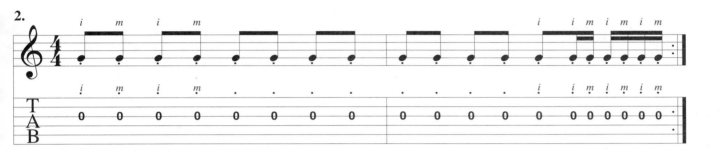

3.

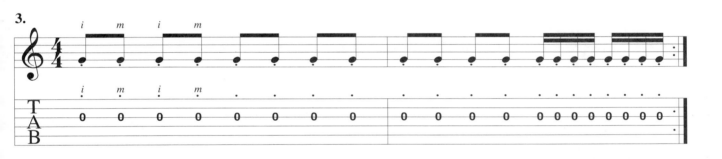

4.

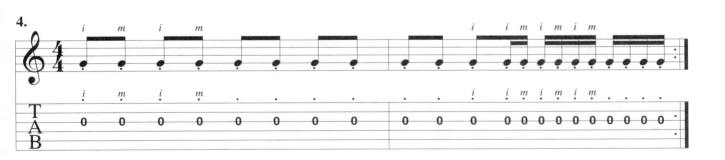

5.

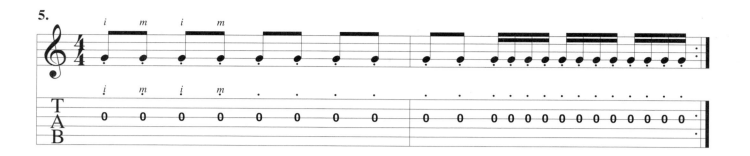

6.

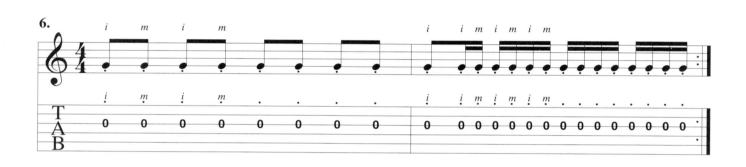

7.

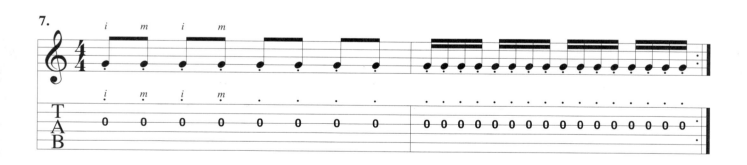

8.

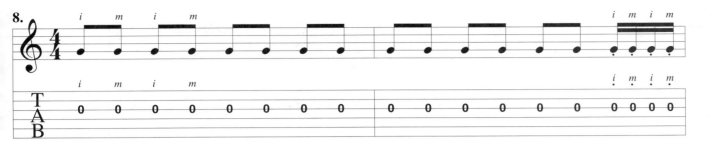

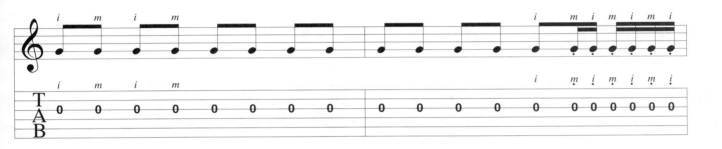

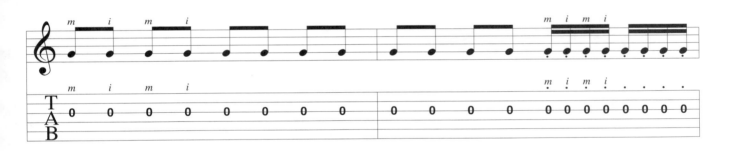

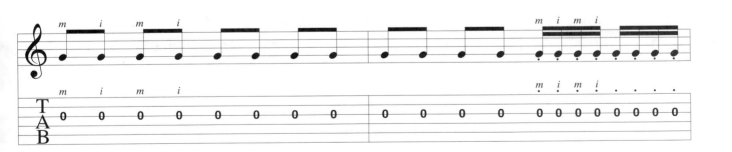

(continued on next page)

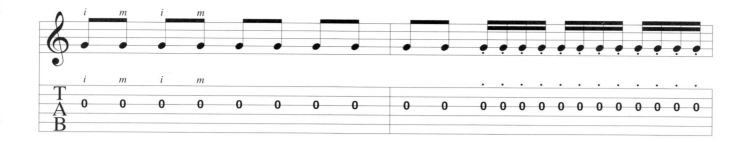

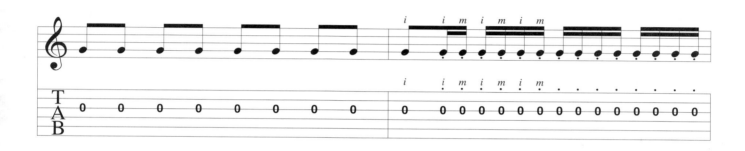

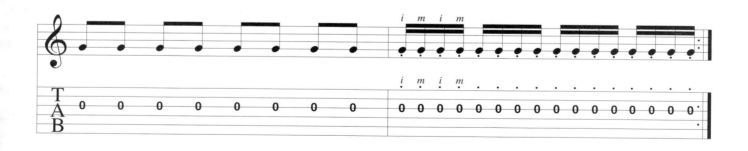

Synchronization

Synchronization means playing the right-hand finger at the exact same time as the left-hand finger. In the exercise that follows, set your tempo with the sixteenth notes in mind. Play as slowly as necessary to remain in control of the sixteenth notes. Push yourself to faster tempos a little at a time. When a passage feels good and in control at a given tempo, turn the metronome up just one notch or two until you reach the desired speed.

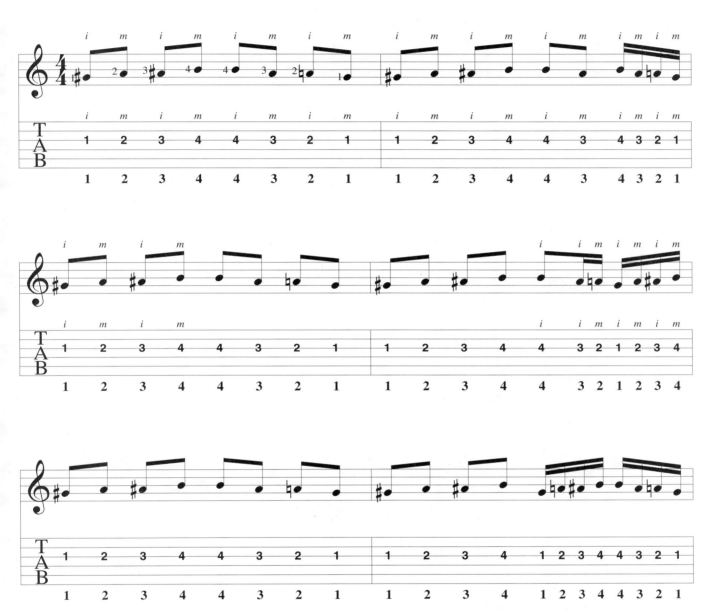

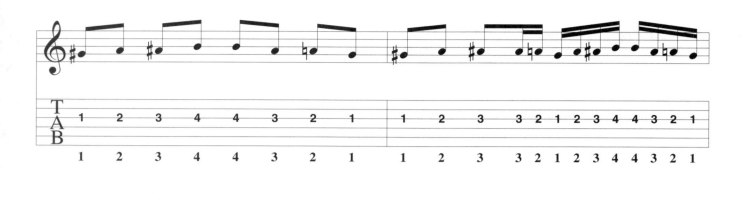

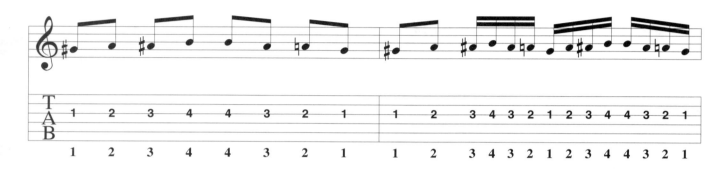

String Crossing

A good deal has already been said about string crossing. It is covered in the "Right-Hand Independence" section on page 41. The exercises presented there are the best ones on which to focus for improving finger accuracy and speed during crossing strings. Also, see the section about marking string crossings on page 90.

Piecing Things Together

Assuming you've been working on your string crossing, the speed bursts are now comfortably speedy, and your hands are synchronized, the most logical thing to do now is to put everything together.

The easiest skill to acquire in the realm of speed is playing fast on one string. The situation that slows us down considerably is having to switch strings. Familiarize yourself with the next little exercise, but don't stop there. Work out all your most difficult scales the same way.

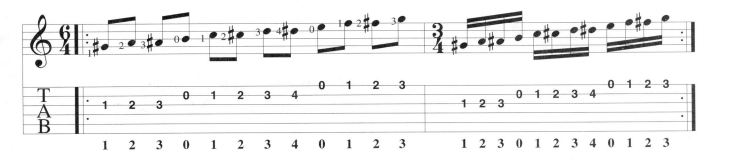

Here is a chromatic scale in groups of three. This is my favorite exercise for working up speed. I particularly like to push this one up one metronome notch at a time. For technical focus, though, *make sure your hands are synchronized!*

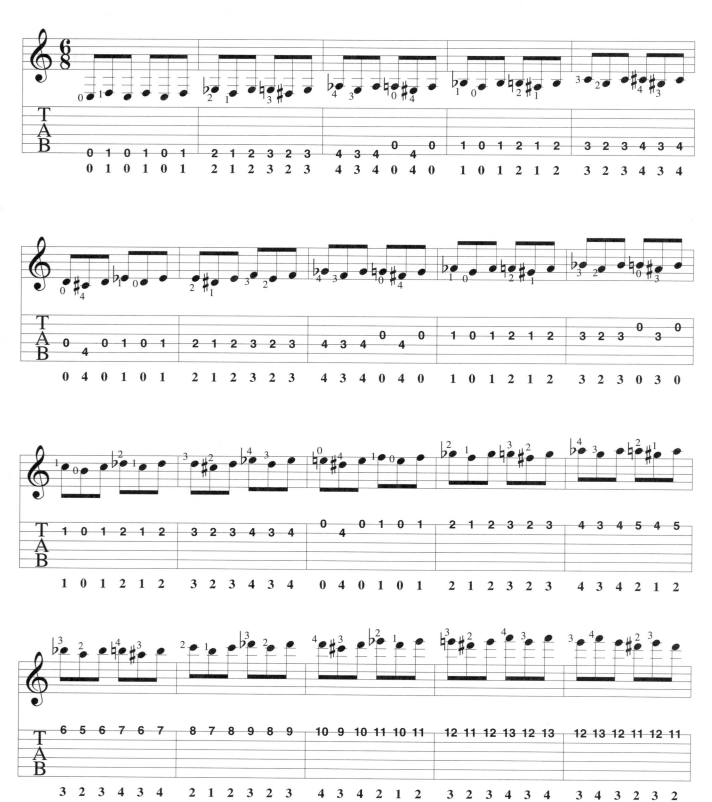

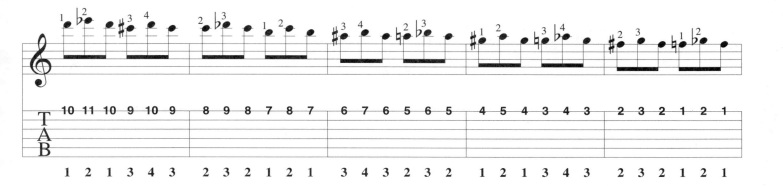

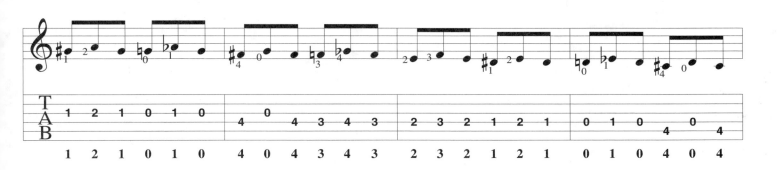

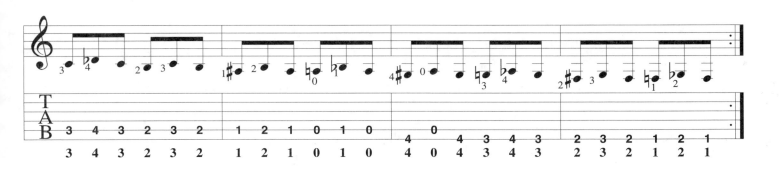

Some Other Speed Aids

Here is a chromatic scale with some rhythmic variations. Practicing scales with various rhythmic variations is invaluable to making them faster and cleaner. Notice that certain rhythmic configurations, including dots, triplets, etc., create short speed burst situations. The variations below are just a few possibilities. Practice them with this chromatic scale fingering. You should apply them to your other scales, as well.

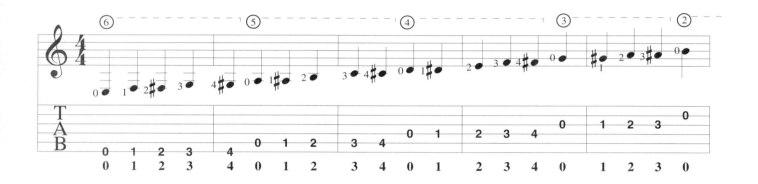

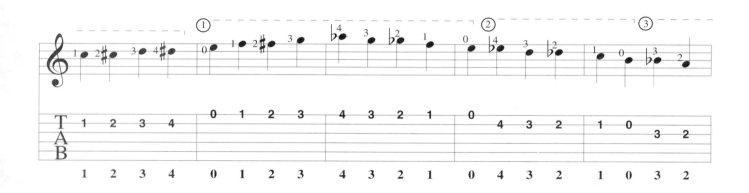

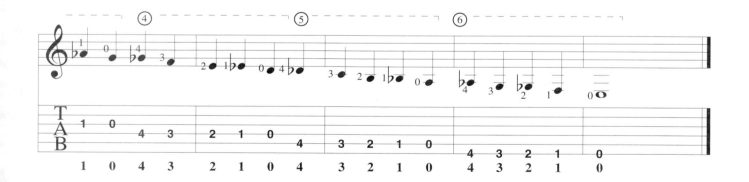

Rhythmic Variations

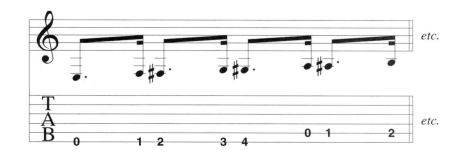

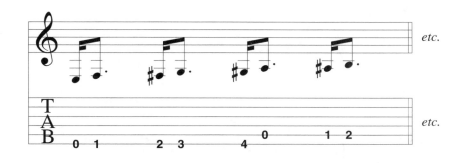

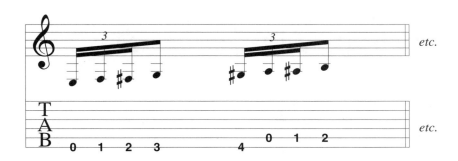

And now, for more fun, try these! Group #1 concentrates on one string, Group #2 on two strings, and in Group #3... anything goes! Remember, you can only go as fast as you can play the sixteenth notes, so work these out slowly. To reap the maximum benefits from these, think before you play every note, and feel each note as you play it.

Speed Bursts

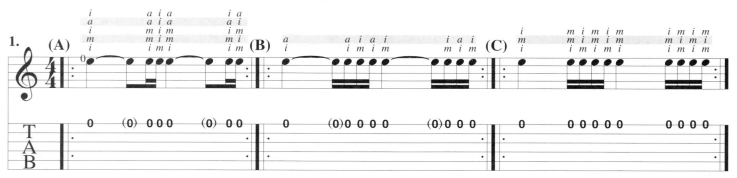

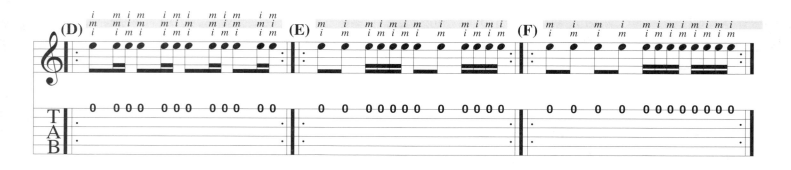

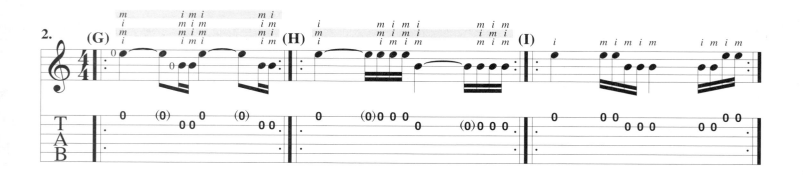

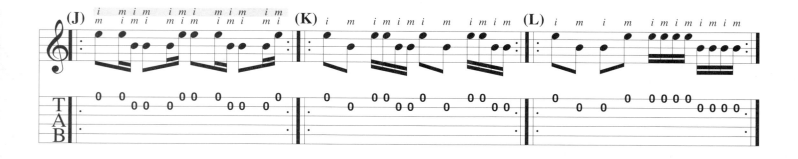

3.

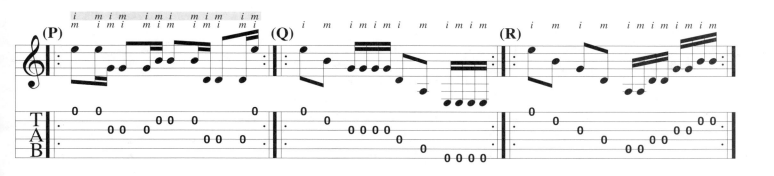

"Sometimes your Joy is the source of your Smile, but sometimes your Smile can be the source of your Joy."

• Thich Nhat Hanh •

Problem Solving in Scales

Everyone is eventually confronted with scales that at first glance seem impossible to play. There is no barrier, though, that cannot be broken down and overcome.

These techniques always work for me, so there is no reason why they should not work for you, too. Basically, I do three things when I want to solve scale problems. They are:

1. Marking the right-hand string crossings (especially the awkward ones).
2. Breaking the scale down into smaller groups (in the case of a longer scale).
3. Using a guide finger in the right hand.

Marking String Crossings

Marking the string crossings refers to knowing when the string changes occur in a scale, and which fingers are crossing. In an ascending scale, *i* to *m* would be best, and *m* to *i* would be more awkward. For instance, when changing from the third to the second strings, it is easiest to change from *i* to *m*. In a descending scale, *m* to *i* is best, and *i* to *m* would be the awkward crossing. For instance, when crossing from the second to the third strings, changing from *m* to *i* is best. So, by marking the string crossings, you are just alerting yourself to exactly what your fingers need to do.

This can be done with the best results by practicing the scale with the right hand alone on open strings, as shown in the following example using the scale from Sor's famous *Opus 9 Variations*:

The scale:

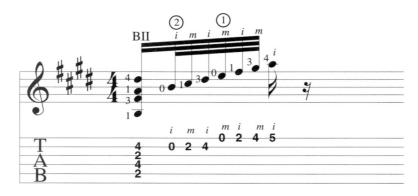

The same scale on open strings:

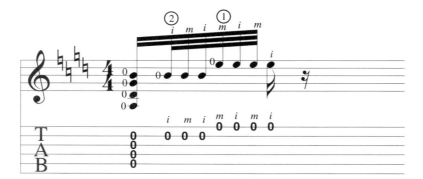

The example that follows shows how a much longer scale can be broken down. The original, #1, is unmeasured and contains 23 notes. In #2 it is taken at a very slow and even pace to get a good feeling for the right-hand fingering, and its open-string pattern is exposed. Exercises #3 and #4 show that when played slowly, it breaks down into groups of four, and accents are added to enable the guide finger (in this case, *i*) to mark every group of four. The guide finger is usually the strongest of the two alternating fingers, and is used to help ease the burden of alternation when we play faster. As we increase the speed, it becomes impossible to think *i-m-i-m-i-m-i-m*, so with *i* as the guide finger, we can now feel *i-i-i-i-i-i-i-i*, and simply let *m* fall in its place. In #5, groups of four notes are added on until we arrive at the whole scale. Since the accents are for technical practice, they are finally taken away.

Evolution of a Scale

from *"Tiento Antiguo"* by **Joaquin Rodrigo**

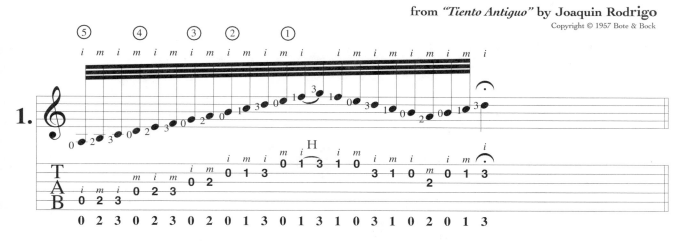

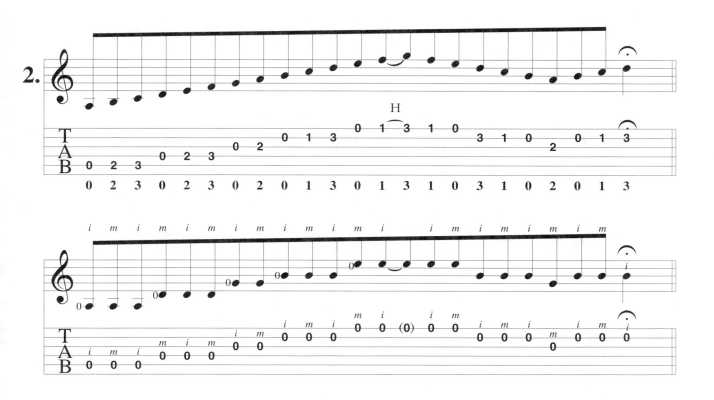

3.

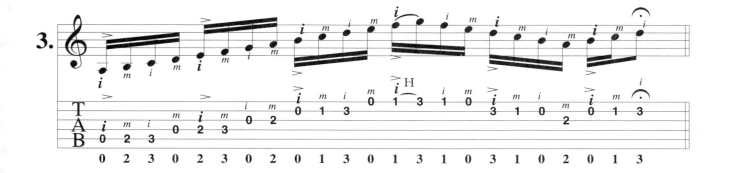

4.

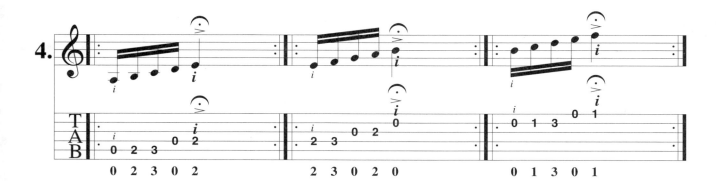

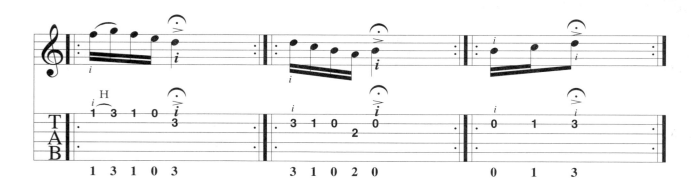

5.

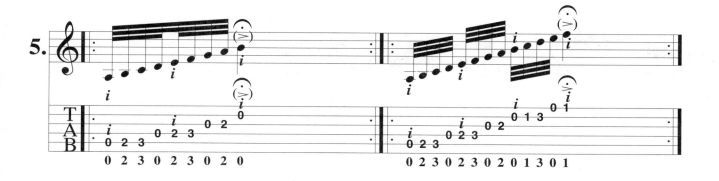

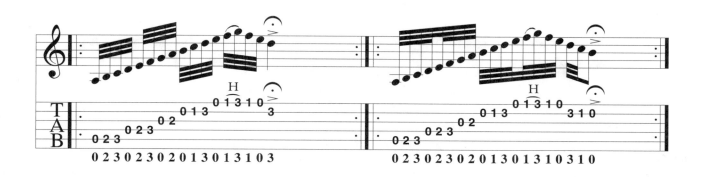

6.

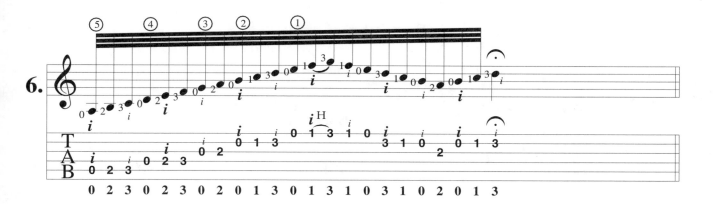

Scale Study—*Double* from the *Courante, Partita No.1*, BWV 1002, Johann Sebastian Bach

This is the *Double* to the *Courante* from Johann Sebastian Bach's *Partita No. 1* (originally in B Minor) for solo violin, BWV 1002. This excerpt is from an arrangement in A Minor I did some time ago. I've also done it in B Minor, but I just liked the sound of it better in A Minor. When I was taking fragments from this movement to practice I discovered it makes an incredible scale study.

I have removed the bass notes that were in the original transcription and changed much of the right and left hand fingering accordingly to further focus the attention on the scales. Some of the cross-string leaps may seem unpleasant at first, but after all, it *is* a study. The bulk of the alternation is between *i* and *m*; however, all the fingerings are only suggestions. I personally use a light rest stroke throughout most of the piece, except on the notes surrounding a bass note played with the thumb. I would suggest practicing as much of it as possible with rest strokes for technical purposes, but with free strokes for musical and stylistic reasons.

Double

J. S. Bach

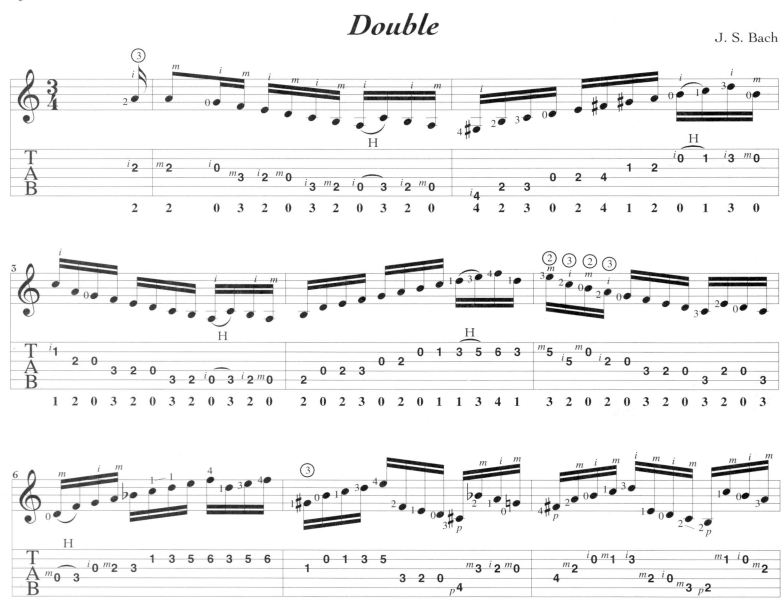

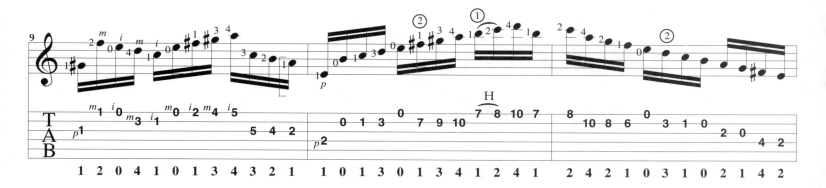

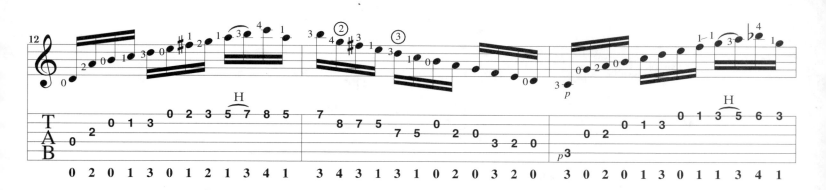

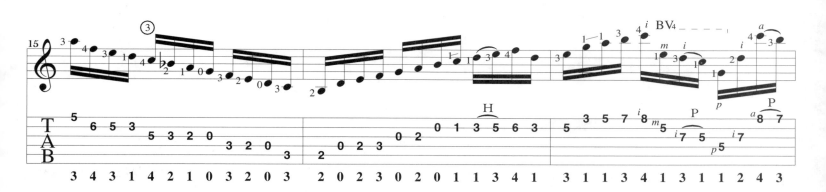

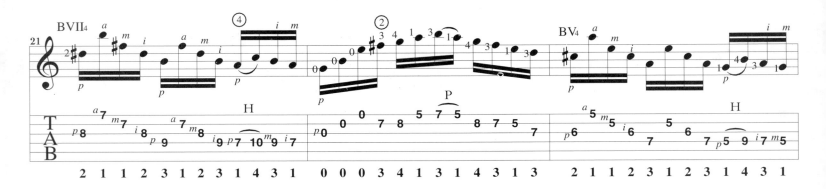

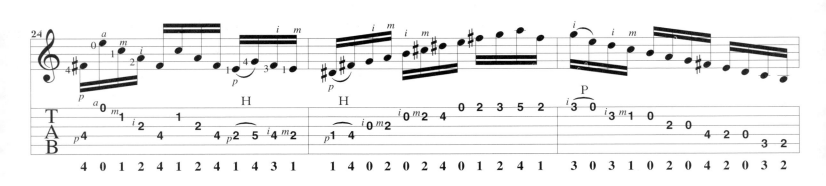

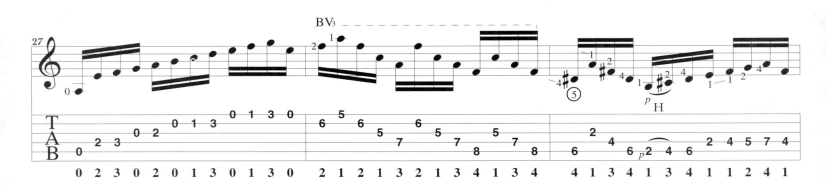

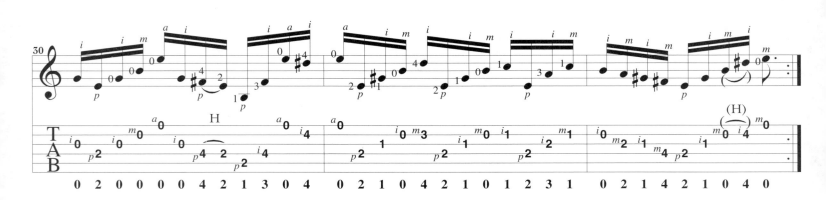

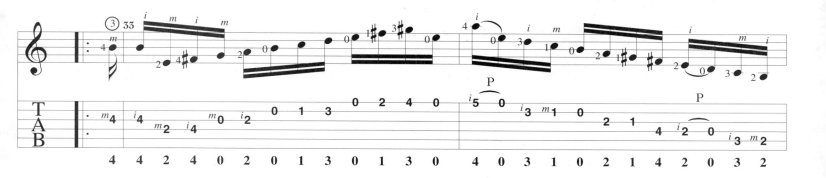

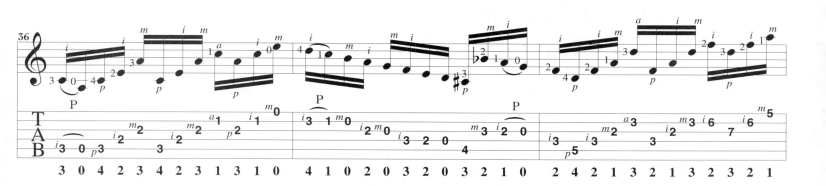

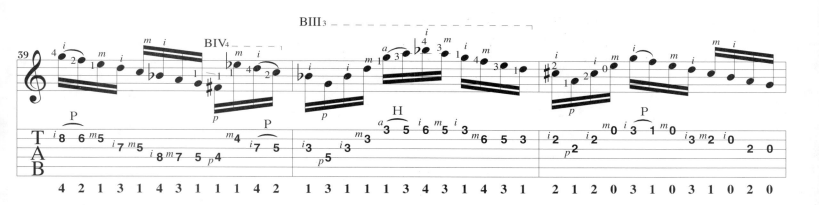

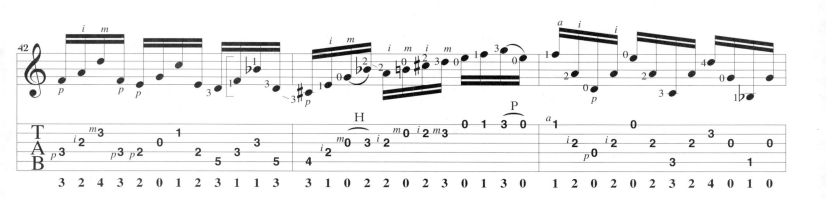

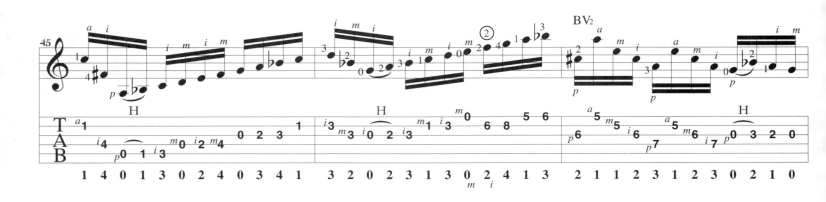

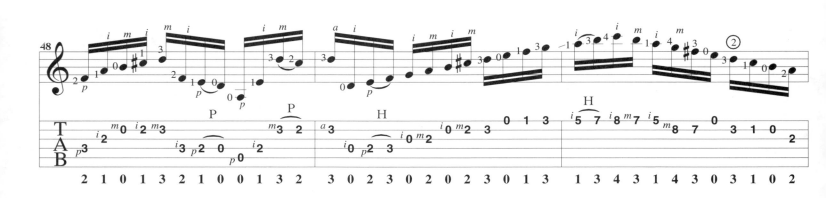

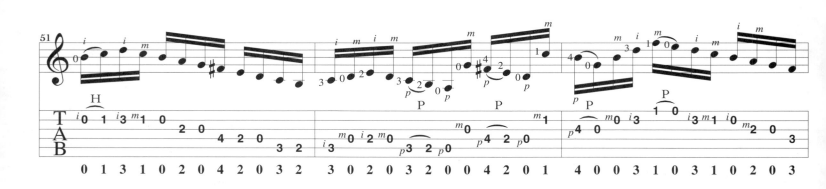

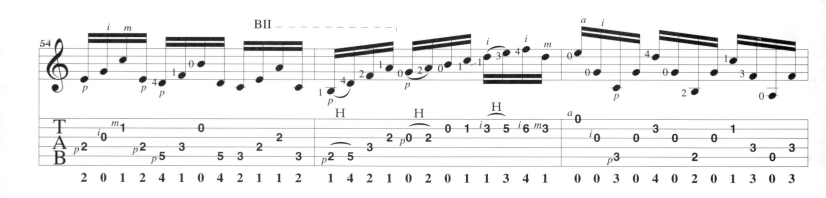

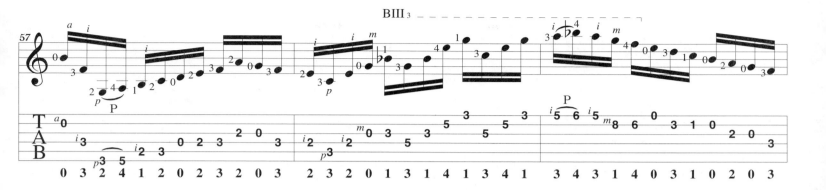

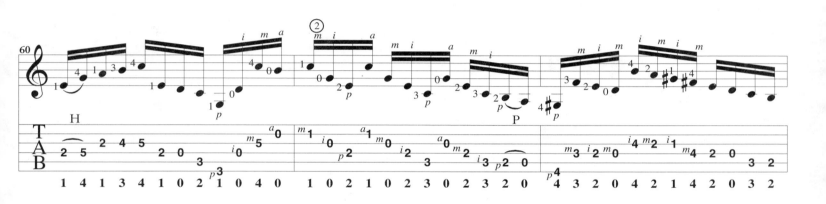

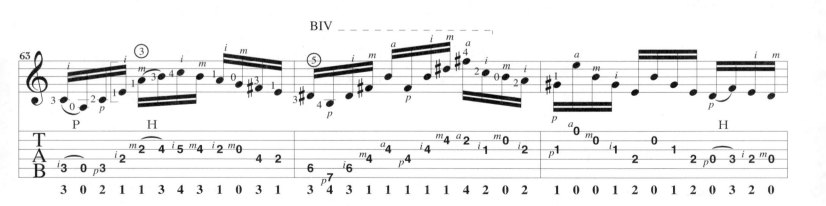

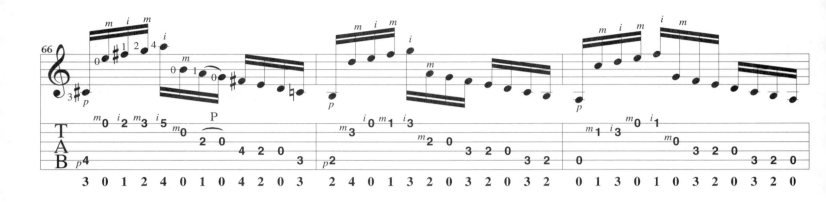

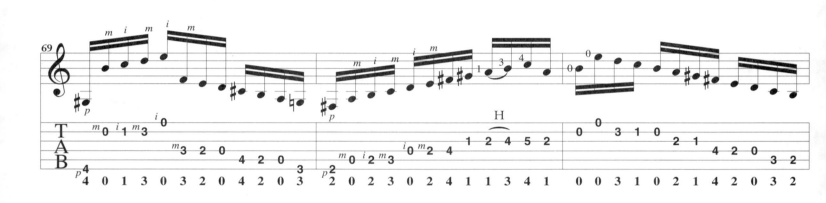

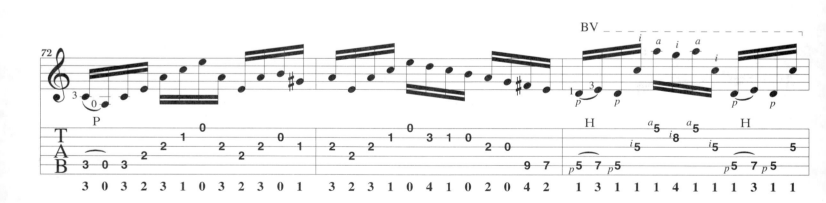

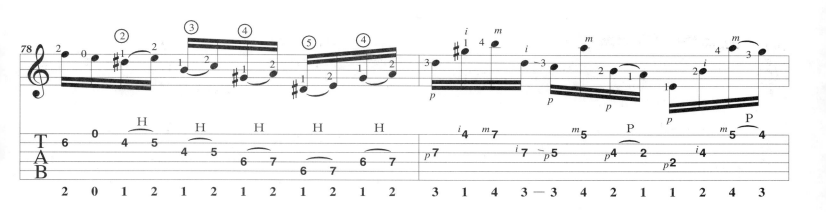

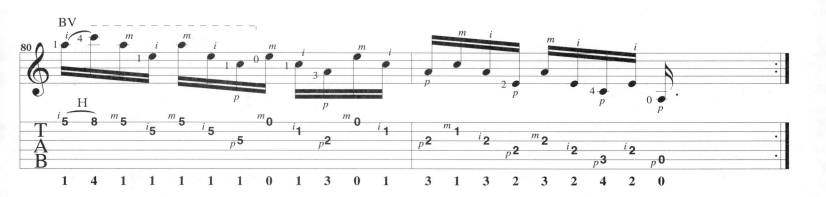

Arpeggios

A few explanations are necessary before you begin to study the many arpeggio patterns provided in this section.

Full Planting and Sequential Planting

There are two ways of preparing the fingers on the strings that facilitate the playing of arpeggios. *Full planting* means that all the fingers involved in an arpeggio (excluding the thumb after the pattern has begun) are planted simultaneously. This is almost exclusively done in ascending arpeggios. Sequential planting involves planting the fingers one at a time, as needed (including the thumb), and is applied to descending arpeggios, and, in practice, most others as well.

Full Plant: Before playing, *p-i-m-a* are placed on the strings. After *a* plays, *p* is planted; after *p* plays, *i-m-a* are planted, and so on.

Sequential Plant: Plant *p*; after it plays, plant *a*; after it plays, plant *m*; after it plays, immediately plant *i*; after it plays, plant *p*, and so on.

Combining full and sequential planting: In an arpeggio that ascends and descends, use a full plant on the ascending portion of the arpeggio, and plant sequentially on the descending portion.

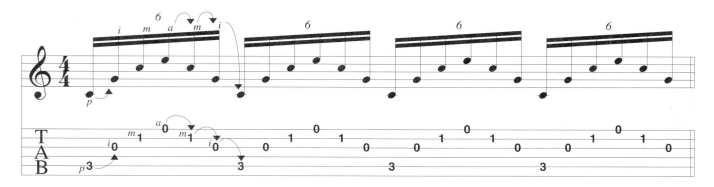

The full plant is most widely used as a training tool for keeping the fingers close to the strings. Since putting all the fingers down at once stops the sound momentarily, it is musically desirable to omit the full plant in many cases. For example, in Matteo Carcassi's *Etude No. 3, Opus 60*, the tempo is so leisurely that employing a full plant on the ascending arpeggio would stop everything from ringing, so using a sequential plant in this piece would be best. But it is invaluable in other situations. For instance, in the fast arpeggio section in *Leyenda*, by Albéniz, using a full plant not only aids the fingers in approaching the necessary speed, but makes the arpeggios sound crisp and articulate.

Giuliani's *120 Right-Hand Studies*

In the *120 Right Hand Studies*, by Mauro Giuliani, both full planting and sequential planting are put to use. I have organized them into ten groups. Over the years, many students have asked me how they should practice these. I have always broken them down into groups so I am presenting them that way here. I have also put them into what I consider to be a more logical order for study.

There has been hesitation on the part of teachers to have their students practice these studies, and for two good reasons. First of all, to have 120 arpeggio studies staring at you from the music stand is a little overwhelming. Where does one begin?! Also, listening to a V-I cadence (the C to G7 chords) over a prolonged period is "cruel and unusual punishment." These two reasons aside, this group of studies is the best and most comprehensive collection of arpeggio formulas I have seen; and, having practiced all of them diligently myself, I know they deliver results!

The studies have been grouped by each arpeggio formula and its variations. Groups 8 and 9 are exceptions, since it appears that Giuliani threw in some extra arpeggios which do not fit with any of the other formulas. Giuliani declared that if one could play all of these studies well, one could successfully play anything he ever wrote. You know, I think I believe him!

Practicing Tips

My first piece of advice to you is to not ignore the very first study. Although it is comprised of just block chords, it functions well at the beginning to help balance the hand. Listen for perfect balance between the voices as you play it, and make sure your strokes and releases are quick and powerful.

Take one group at a time to practice; not necessarily all in one session, but take your time and feel secure with each before moving on to the next. If one or more patterns in a group are naturally easy for you, bypass them in favor of those that are difficult. Also, feel free to play different chords, or even open strings, as long as the patterns stay the same.

In a short time, after you have practiced them all you will, no doubt, have compiled a mental list of those that give you problems. Work on those daily. You can also select one from each group, and practice the studies in that way. Go ahead—get started!

The Left Hand

Since the point of these studies is right-hand development, the left hand is intentionally repetitive and easy. All of the studies use the same two chords, C and G7. If you are familiar with the chord voicings shown below, you hold the keys to the left hand in the Giuliani studies.

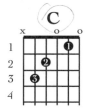 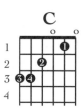  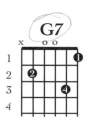

Group #1

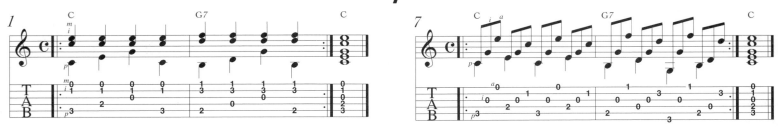

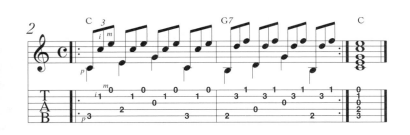

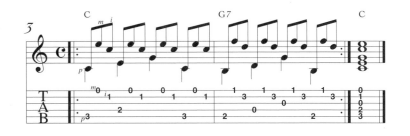

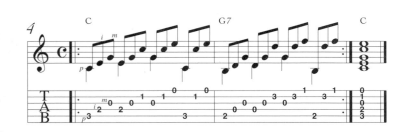

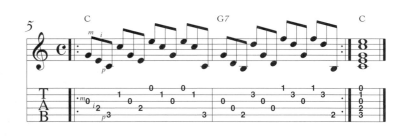

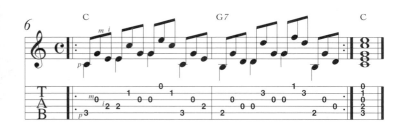

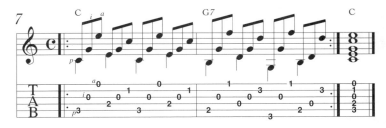

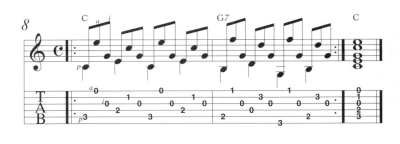

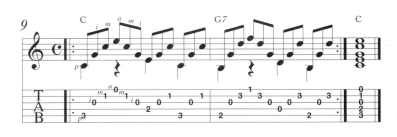

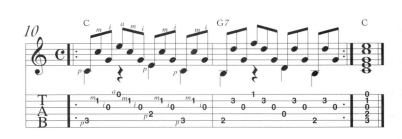

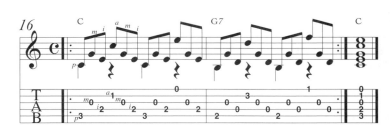

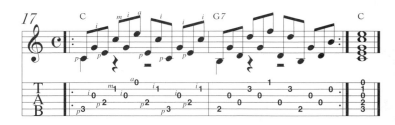

Group #2

(continued on
next page)

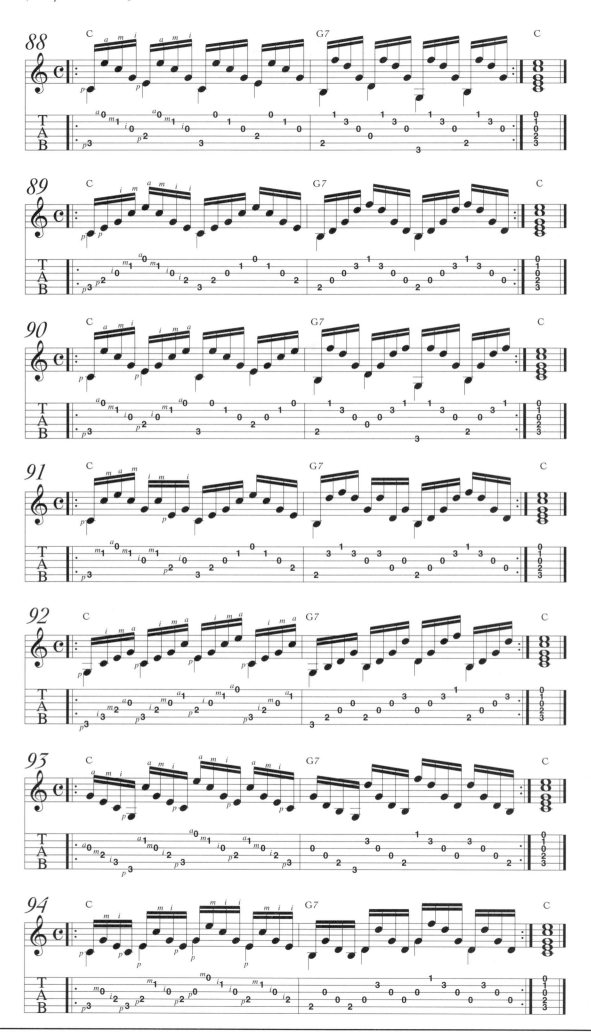

Group #3

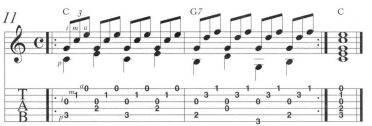

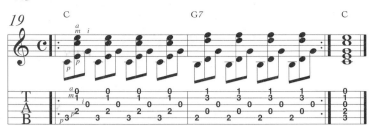

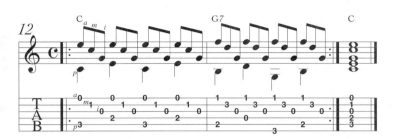

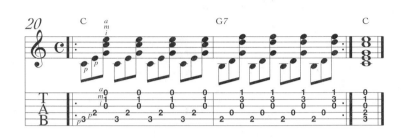

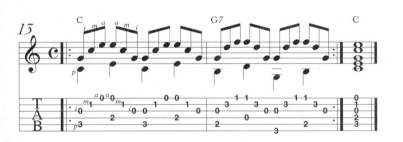

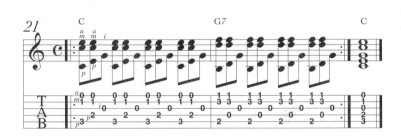

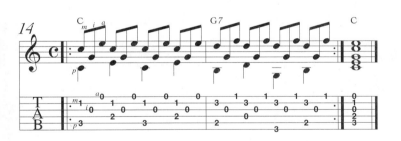

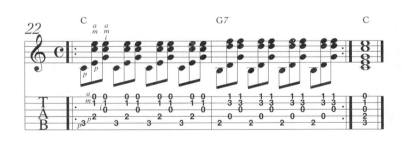

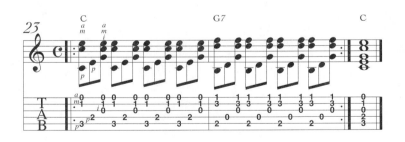

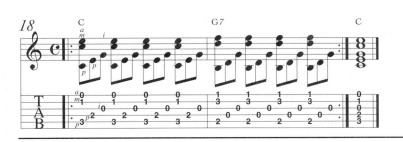

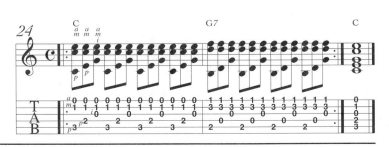

Group #4

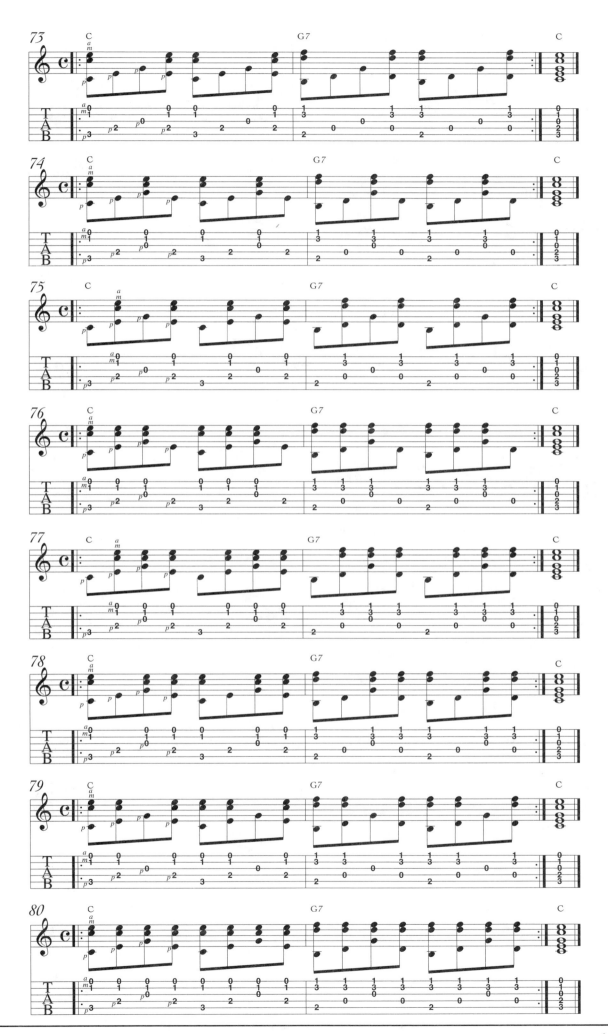

Group #5

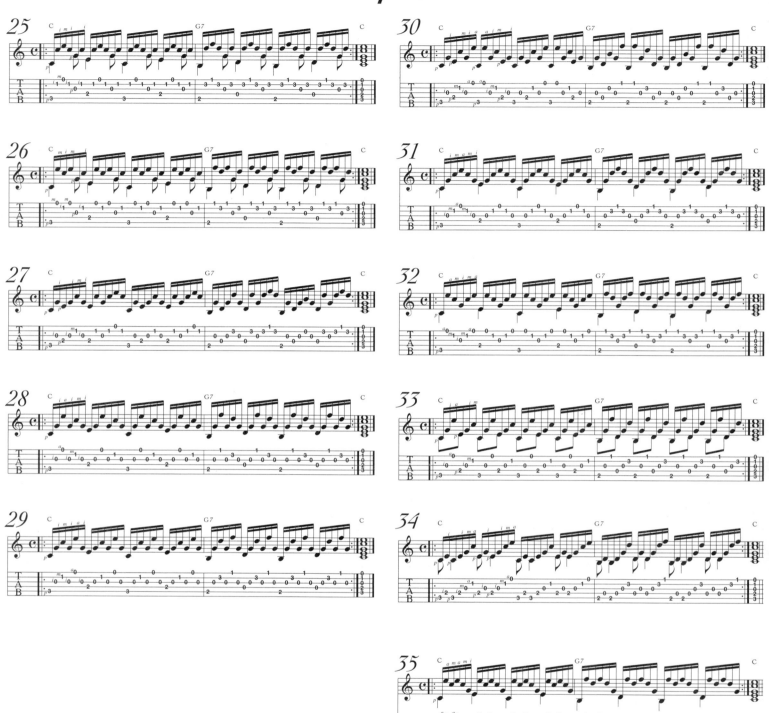

Group #6

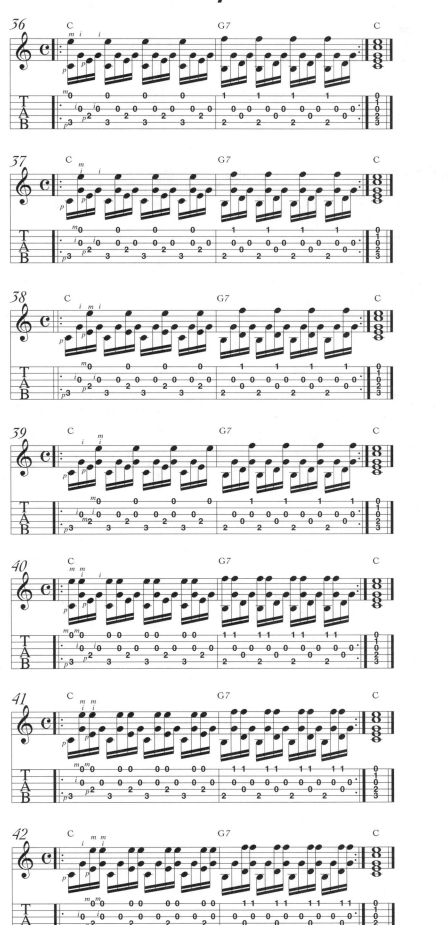

(continued on next page)

43
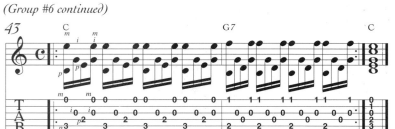

48
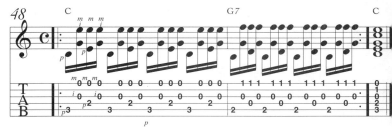

44
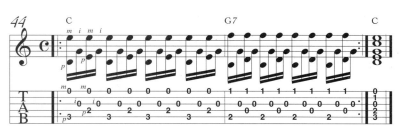

49
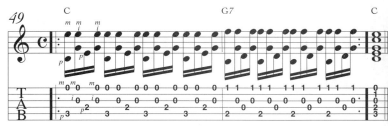

45
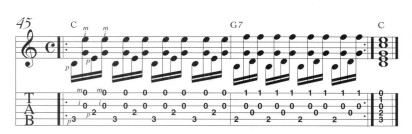

50
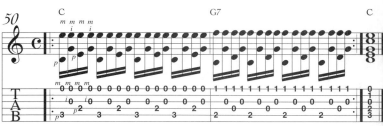

46
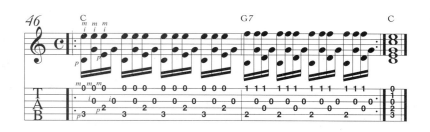

47
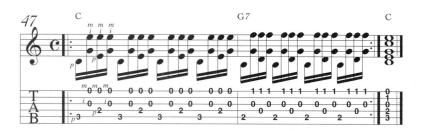

Group #7

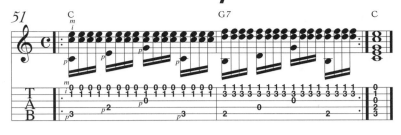

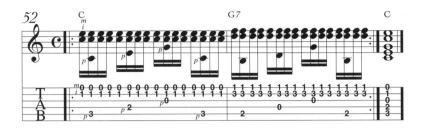

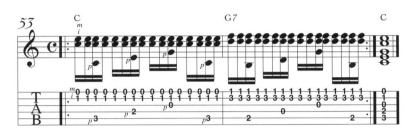

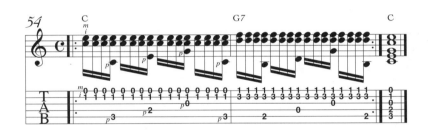

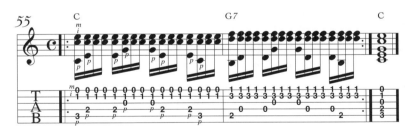

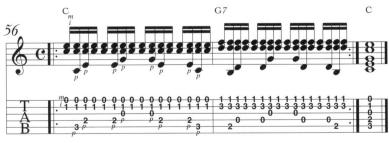

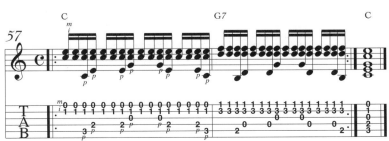

(continued on next page)

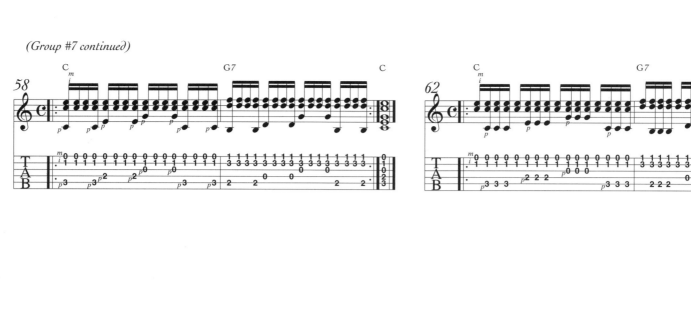

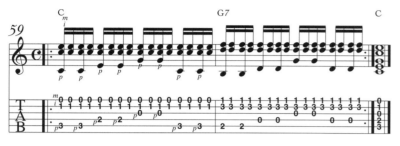

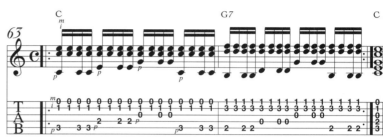

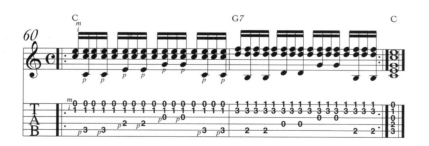

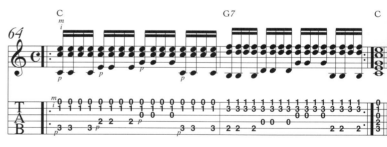

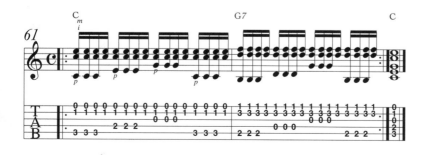

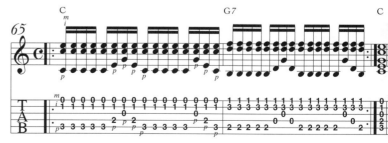

Group #8

95
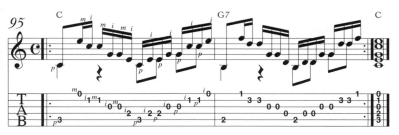

99
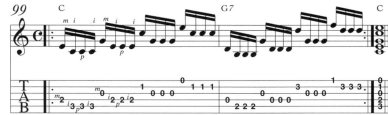

96
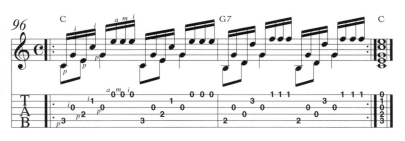

100
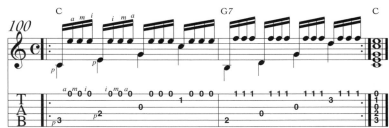

97
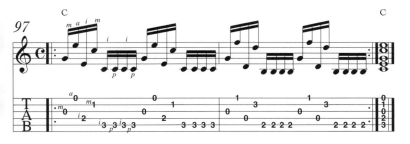

101
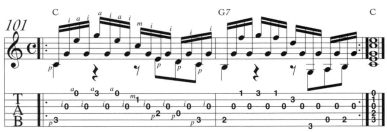

98
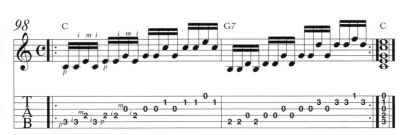

102

(continued on next page)

103

107

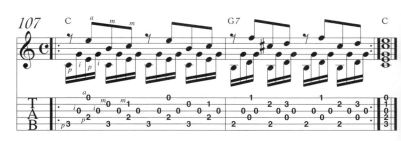

104

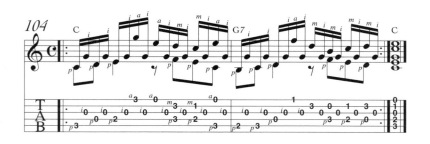

108

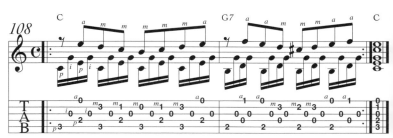

105

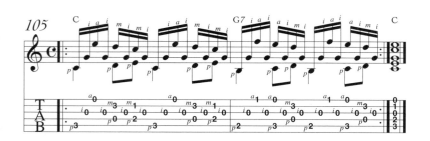

109

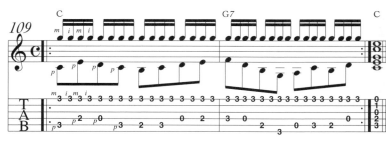

106

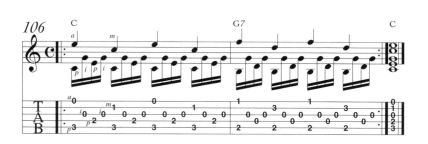

110

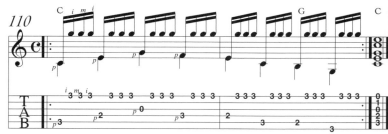

Group #9

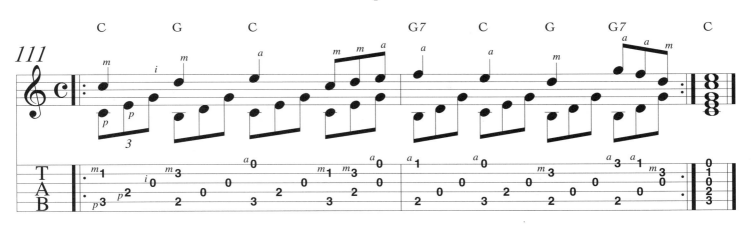

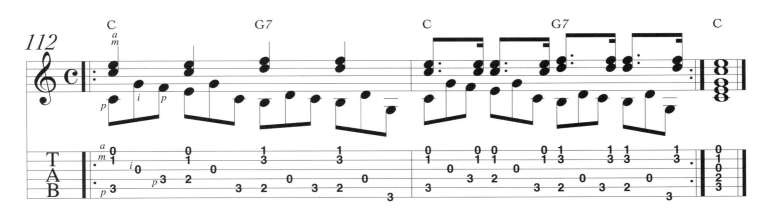

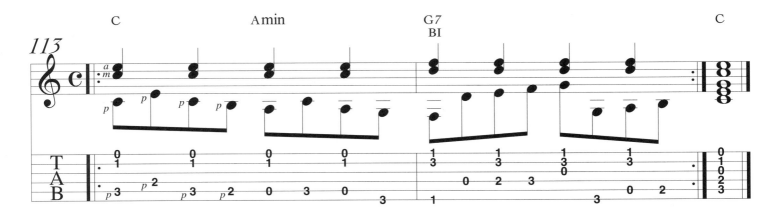

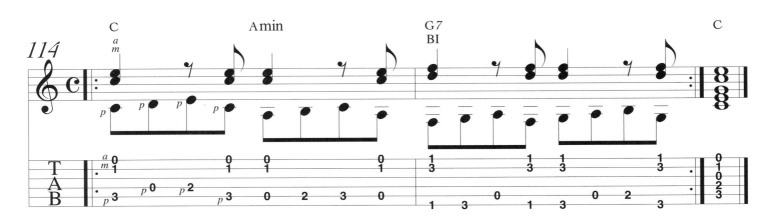

Group #10

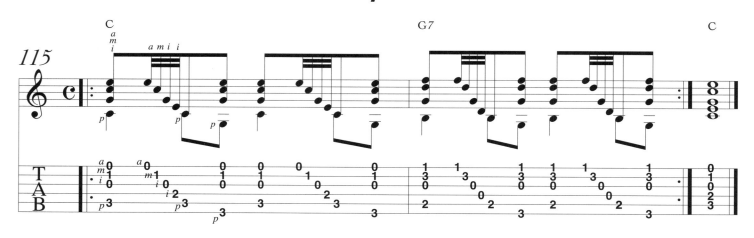

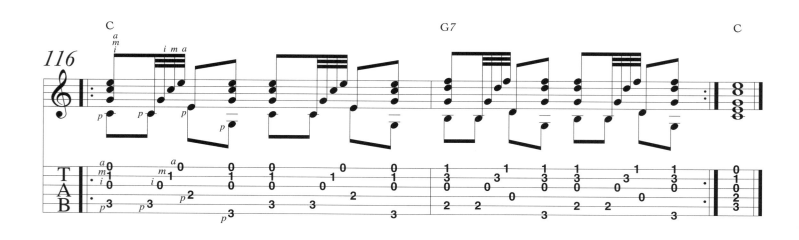

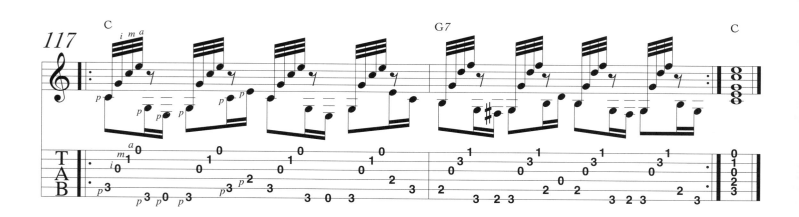

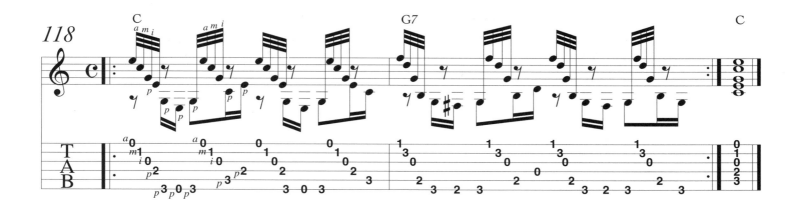

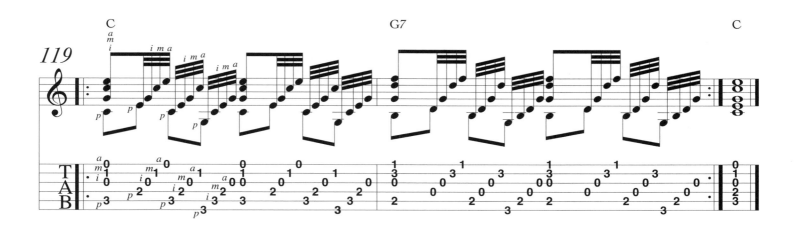

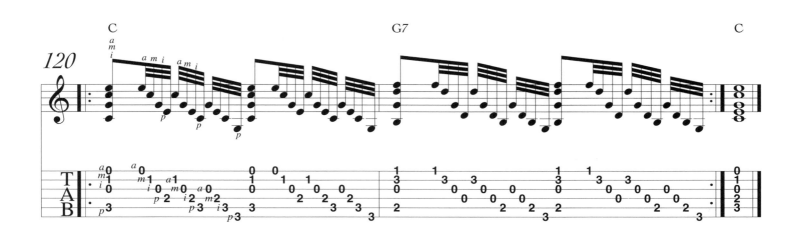

Didactic Doodle by Andrew York

Here is an arpeggio piece that will give anyone a run for their money! Thus far in the arpeggio section of this book, there have been plenty of opportunities to practice a particular pattern over and over again. Andy's *Didactic Doodle* deliberately strings together several challenging arpeggio patterns, none of them lasting for more than a few bars.

Here are some important things to remember:

1. Work on each pattern by itself, first:

   Pattern 1—measures 1 and 2 (5 and 6)
   Pattern 2—measure 7
   Pattern 3—measure 8
   Pattern 4—measure 9
   Pattern 5—measure 10

   Pattern 6—measures 12 and 13
   Pattern 7—measure 15
   Pattern 8—measures 16, l8 and 20
   Pattern 9—measures 17, 19 and 21
   Pattern 10—measures 22 and 23
   Pattern 11—measures 25, 26, 27, and 28

2. Piece them together gradually.

3. Work the accents into the patterns as you practice them individually.

Didactic Doodle

Andrew York

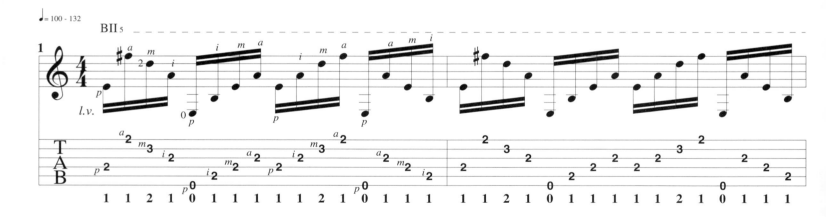

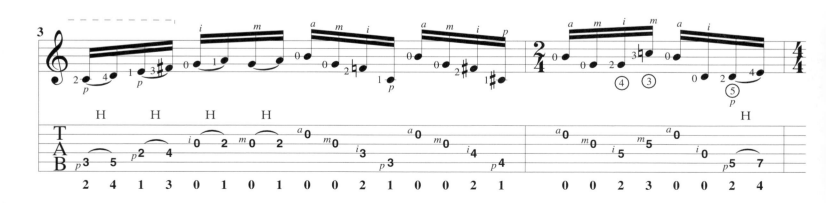

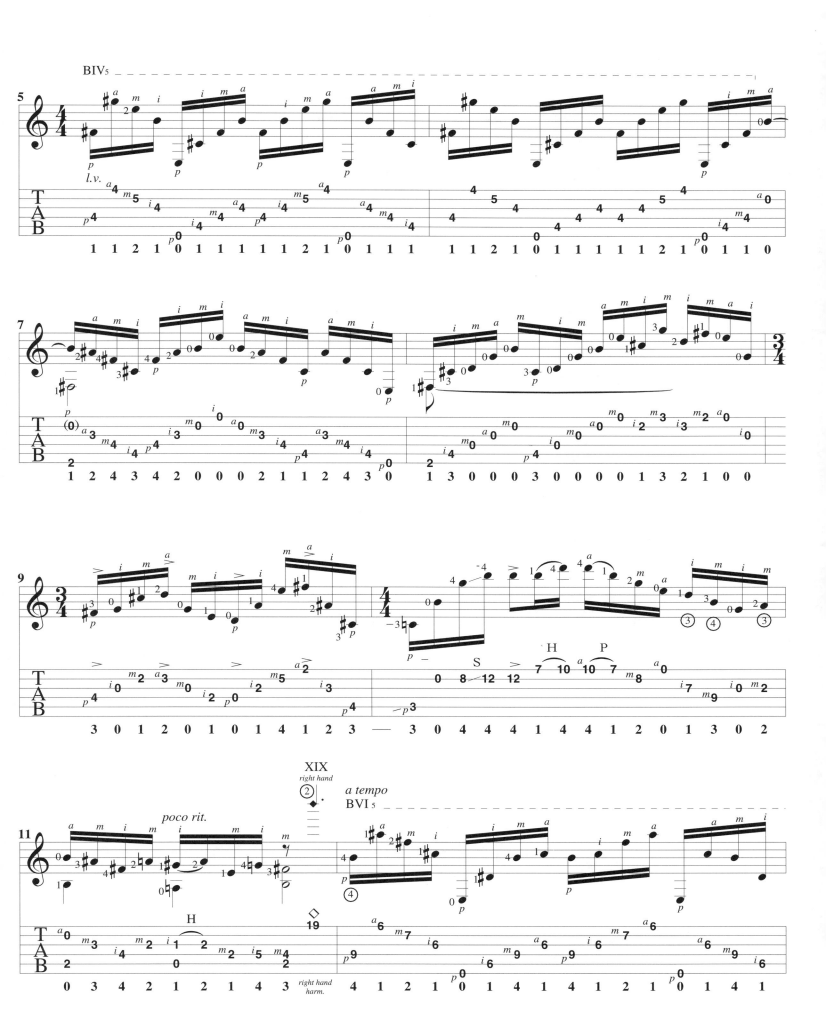

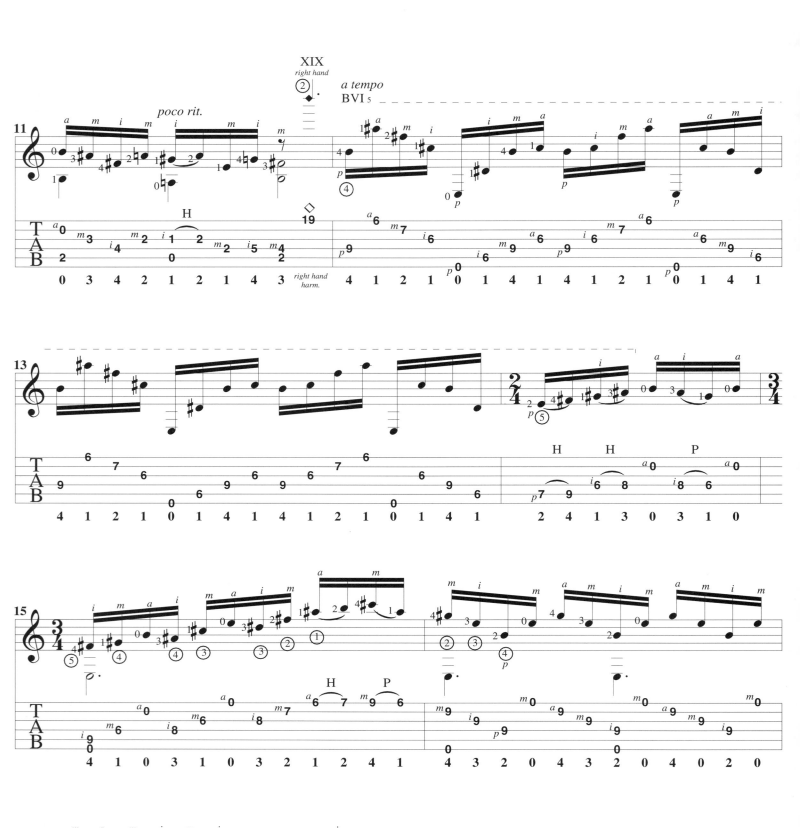

Afterword

Performance Anxiety

There is no substitute for preparation. Being well prepared for a performance gives us the confidence and the self-assurance we need to "go on with the show." However, no matter how well we prepare in advance, there is always that last-minute anxiety from the feeling that we didn't do enough. I think we've all felt this at one time or another, and probably practiced and played the instrument all day the day of the concert, only to feel tired, more insecure, and even more nervous than before! As a result of a tough situation I found a solution for myself that may work for you, too.

It happened when I had to give two concerts for the same organization. The first one was in the evening and the second one was the next afternoon. The entire day before the first performance I had absolutely nothing scheduled, and decided I would just take my time and go slowly through the entire program. I thought I was using my time wisely, but as I practiced, I found little things in the music were giving me problems which had not bothered me before. OH NO!!! My mental composure continued on a downward slide the rest of the day. By the time I settled in for my pre-concert nap I was a mess! Needless to say, I napped not. At the concert that night, I had several memory slips, among some other small problems. With my self-confidence shattered, I awaited the next day's recital.

The following day I arose late and had little time for breakfast. Since the concert was out in the country somewhere, my hosts informed me we would leave right away to allow plenty of time. It was just time enough, because we arrived at the venue only ten minutes before the downbeat. I sat up my things on the stage, went back and tuned up, and rushed out on stage and played one of my best concerts ever!

The lesson: not only did I not have time that day to play, warm up, or even think about the concert, I also *didn't have time to worry about it*. Nowadays I actually play the guitar very little the day of a concert. I'll just tune up that morning, make sure my strings sound alright, and touch-up my nails if they need it. I try to stay in a normal and "happy" frame of mind. If I'm not happy, I find a way to make myself happy. I'll read, watch something funny on TV, think of things I like doing, go for a walk, call someone on the phone; or anything else that seems like it will do the trick. I try to take a short nap (just fifteen to thirty minutes or so) before I leave for the concert . This clears my head. Backstage, just before the concert, I remind myself of a few things:

1. I think, "This is great! I can't wait to play!" After all, this is what I've wanted to do all my life.
2. I think of what the program is; or better still, I like to have one in front of me to review while I warm up.
3. I warm up with light exercises only: stretches, short scales, and/or selections from the Daily Warm-Up Routine in this book. I don't "run through" anything.
4. I let myself feel my nervousness and don't try to get rid of my nerves anymore, or "freak out" when I am nervous. I just expect to be nervous. As with the airline attendants who endlessly hassle me about taking my guitar on board, I have learned to confront nerves on their terms and with confidence. By feeling my nervousness, I'm accepting the fact that I am nervous; but acknowledge only the physical signs, such as a fast heart rate, sweating, lack of sufficient oxygen or even nausea. I focus on each one individually for a few seconds. Some form of steady deep breathing (see description next page) almost always helps these symptoms subside. I refuse to let them conquer me. Unlike the airline attendants, most of the nerves eventually go away! I convert the remaining nerves into excitement about playing the concert. I think to myself, "No more endless repetitions of these pieces; all I have to do is run everything once and that's it! How easy!"

I like to remind myself of something my teacher, Pepe Romero, told me when I was fourteen: "No matter what, the sun always comes out the next day and life goes on." After all, the troubles didn't matter at all, and somebody most certainly walked out of the concert happier than before!

5. Then, I go out on stage and just go for it. I let my "inner player" play the concert for me; that player we all have inside us which usually emerges when we're playing in front of the TV watching old Star Trek re-runs or the NCAA playoffs!

Also don't forget that without being nervous we produce very little adrenaline. Playing a concert without being at least a little nervous makes for a lackluster performance.

A Simple Deep Breathing Routine
Inhale deeply and observe how you feel as you you hold your breath. Then, fully and slowly exhale while expelling your nerves out with the breath.

Practice

Always practice with a purpose. Practicing without a purpose is like a broken pencil: pointless. Have a clear idea of what you need to practice. Organize the hierarchy of items you want to improve upon. Some are long-term (such as practicing the *Concierto de Aranjuez*) and within those long-term goals are smaller goals (such as improving your tone) that can be accomplished in one or two practice sessions.

Remember that whenever you play a note on the guitar you have two choices: to improve or go downhill. If you practice without getting anything done, you've either not concentrated hard enough or put too many things on the menu for the day. Next time, focus on smaller goals. Allowing yourself to make even a bad tone on the instrument without taking steps to correct it is not acceptable. Any chance you waste to play something well is a step downhill. There is always something on which you can improve, no matter how small, whenever you pick up the instrument. There is practice and there is playing (going for it). The common thread between the two is the simple discipline we cultivate of striving for that little glimmer of excellence.

Inspiration

Inspiration only lasts a relatively brief time. We all eventually find ourselves experiencing a "dry spell." We get stuck on something in our practicing and can't seem to improve, and sometimes it may seem that we're getting worse. At times we may even think of just quitting. Have you ever felt that the joy you once had for playing is gone forever?

These are not emotions you're experiencing alone. They visit everyone now and then. Occasionally we need to give ourselves a break and put down the guitar for a day, a few days, or however long it takes to feel refreshed again. For those who play for a living and don't always have that luxury, some digging back into one's past might be the key. Why did you want to play the guitar in the first place? Try to recall the feelings you experienced when you first decided that you really wanted to play. Perhaps recall the joy you felt when you heard that first recording or concert that thrilled you. What qualities about the instrument first drew you to it?

As I have done for several circumstances in my life, it may make you feel better to jot down a few of these positive thoughts on a piece of paper. Then, when you hit another rough period, you can read through them.

In Conclusion

Music is the most powerful of all the arts. It instantly stirs up emotions, conjures visions, and offers glimpses of other, higher dimensions. It arouses men to battle; kindles amorous passions in lovers; soothes a baby to sleep; comforts us when we grieve. It engages our hearts and our minds, and can bring out the best that we are. One can safely presume that not a single emotion, nor any human or natural event, has been left undocumented by music.

As musicians, our objective is to command the elements of music as best we can in order to tap into that other dimension. It is our access into heaven, if only for a while. But while we are there we can take all who are listening with us. If just one person is uplifted by our playing and walks away feeling better than before he came, we have made a difference. A healing has taken place.

I very much hope that you have found at least one thing in this book that has helped you. I also hope that, as you work to improve your technique, you do not lose sight of the larger goals: to be able to express yourself freely on your instrument and to turn every note you play into great music. When you can do those things, you cease to be just a guitar player and become a healer and magician.

Scott Tennant

Scott Tennant's reputation as a brilliant performer has been established worldwide. His accolades include becoming the first American ever to be awarded first prize in the Tokyo International Guitar Competition in 1989, a silver-medal performances in both the 1988 Concours International de Guitare of Radio France in Paris, and winning 1984 Toronto International Competition.

He has recorded the complete guitar works of Joaquin Rodrigo for GHA Records. He also records for Delos records, and is on the guitar faculties of the National Guitar Summer Workshop and the University of Southern California.

Born in Detroit in 1962, Scott began playing the guitar at six years of age. During his Junior High and High School years, he studied classical guitar with Lee Dyament, Joe Fava and flamenco with Juan Serrano. He also played the bass trombone in his high school concert band, and the violin in the school orchestra.

("These instruments made the biggest impression on my dog, Skippy," Scott recalled, "who I think must have developed some nervous disorder because of my practicing at home. He loved the sound of the guitar, but hated my violin and trombone playing. It made him shiver and growl.")

Scott moved to Los Angeles in 1980 to attend the University of Southern California, where he studied with Pepe Romero and James Smith. It was during this time that the L. A. Guitar Quartet was formed (then the U.S.C. Guitar Quartet), and he has been touring and recording with the group ever since. As a student there, he performed in the master classes of such luminaries as Joaquin Rodrigo and Andrés Segovia.